101
Quotable
Christians

*More Than 2,000 Memorable Thoughts
from People Who Shaped Your Faith*

10666595

BARBOUR
PUBLISHING

Published by Barbour Books, an imprint of Barbour Publishing, Inc., P.O. Box 719, Uhrichsville, Ohio 44683, www.barbourbooks.com

Our mission is to publish and distribute inspirational products offering exceptional value and biblical encouragement to the masses.

ecpa Member of the
Evangelical Christian
Publishers Association

Printed in the United States of America.

CONTENTS

Born in 1954 in Portland, Oregon, Randy Alcorn gave his life to Christ in high school. At age twenty-two, he cofounded the Good Shepherd Church in Boring, Oregon.

He split his time between family, ministry, writing, and activism. After his faith-driven protests led to arrests, he gave up his ministry position to spare the church embarrassment, depending on his writing for a living. The income from his books was dedicated to his Eternal Perspective Ministries, emphasizing pro-life projects and good works such as famine relief.

He is the author of more than forty books, including *50 Days of Heaven: Reflections That Bring Eternity to Light*, *Safely Home*, and *Courageous*. His books have been translated into more than thirty languages with sales in excess of seven million copies.

Tomorrow's character is made out of today's thoughts. Temptation may come suddenly, but sin doesn't.

The fear of God is a profound respect for his holiness, which includes a fear of the consequences of disobeying Him.

The Purity Principle (2003)

The act of giving is a vivid reminder that it's all about God, not about us. It's saying I am not the point. He is the point. He does not exist for me. I exist for Him.

If we give instead of keep, if we invest in the eternal instead of the temporal, we store up treasures in heaven that will never stop paying dividends. Whatever treasures we store up on earth will be left behind when we leave. Whatever treasures we store up in heaven will be waiting for us when we arrive.

The Treasure Principle (2001)

The cost of redemption cannot be overstated. The wonders of grace cannot be overemphasized. Christ took the hell He didn't deserve so we could have the heaven we don't deserve.

In Christianity, men gain righteousness only by confessing their unrighteousness and being covered by Christ's merit. Every other religion is man working his way to God. Christianity is God working His way to men.

The Grace and Truth Paradox (2003)

Don't forget that the most effective form of child abuse is giving a child everything they want.

Lord Foulgrin's Letters (2001)

God comes right out and tells us why He gives us more money than we need. It's not so we can find more ways to spend it. It's not so we can indulge ourselves and spoil our children. It's not so we can insulate ourselves from needing God's provision. It's so we can give and give generously (2 Corinthians 8:14; 9:11).

Abundance isn't God's provision for me to live in luxury. It's His provision for me to help others live. God entrusts me with His money not to build my kingdom on earth, but to build His kingdom in heaven.

Money, Possessions, and Eternity (2003)

The conflicting missions of the two armies seemed to have no fog, no gray, only black-and-white clarity. I had lived my life in terms of compromise, rule-bending, trade-offs, concessions, bargaining, striking deals, finding middle ground. In these two great armies, there was no such thing. Good was good, and evil was evil, and they shared no common ground.

Edge of Eternity (1999)

Heaven isn't an extrapolation of earthly thinking; earth is an extension of heaven, made by the Creator King.

Earth is an in-between world touched by both heaven and hell. Earth leads directly into heaven or directly into hell, affording a choice between the two. The best of life on earth is a glimpse of heaven; the worst of life is a glimpse of hell.

Heaven (2004)

The problem of evil and suffering is the most common reason people give for not believing in God.

When we examine the Bible's perspective on evil, we learn that its essence is a refusal to accept the true God as God. Instead, evil elevates someone or something else in God's place. This is an act of idolatry and rebellion against God.

If God Is Good: Why Do We Hurt? (2010)

Real gold fears no fire.

Safely Home (2011)

Often God has wiped away my own tears as I've contemplated potentially faith-jarring situations. I've been left not in despair, but with great hope that defies description and a peace that transcends understanding.

In times of crisis we try to make sense of life. We crave perspective for our minds and relief for our hearts. We need our worldview realigned by God's inspired Word.

If God Is Good: Faith in the Midst of Suffering and Evil (2009)

Make no mistake—one of Satan's favorite tactics is feeding us an unworthy, dull, and distorted view of heaven. He knows we'll lack motivation to tell others about Jesus when our view of heaven isn't that much better than our concept of hell.

Every human heart yearns for not only a person but a place. The place we were made for. The place made for us.

In Light of Eternity: Perspectives on Heaven (1999)

While exploring God's goodness in the midst of a suffering world, I've taken the most pleasure in focusing on Him, exploring His attributes of goodness, love, holiness, justice, patience, grace, and mercy.

You and I are characters in God's story, handmade by Him. Every character serves a purpose. God loves a great story, and all of us who know Him will recall and celebrate and continue to live in that story for all eternity.

Ninety Days of God's Goodness (2011)

We are God's money managers. He wants us to invest His money in His kingdom. He tells us He's keeping track of every cup of cold water we give the needy in His name. He promises He will reward us in heaven because we help the poor and needy who cannot pay us back for what we do for them.

When you give, it is for *your* good too.

The Law of Rewards (2003)

ARTHUR, KAY

Born in 1933 in Jackson, Michigan, Kay married Jack Arthur in 1965. The couple spent the next three years doing missionary work.

A Bible study group for teenagers that Kay hosted in the Arthur home eventually grew into Precept Ministries International. Based on the "inductive Bible study method," the ministry also produces a television program (*Precepts for Life*) with a reach of some 75 million homes. The National Religious Broadcasters organization has twice presented the program its "Best Television Teaching" award.

Kay Arthur's books include *A Marriage without Regrets, His Imprint: My Expression,* and *Lord, I Need Grace to Make It Today.*

☜

Ultimately, the goal of personal Bible study is a transformed life and a deep and abiding relationship with Jesus Christ.

When you know what God says, what He means, and how to put His truths into practice, you will be equipped for every circumstance of life.

How to Study Your Bible (1994)

His words are truth—not lies, like the enemy's. They're the daily bread which nourishes our soul so we can confront and manage each day and all that He allows that day to bring.

The problem is that so often we forget that we are in warfare and that Satan's target is our mind.

Speak to My Heart, God (1993)

We're so occupied with today that we take no thought for our future and eternity—that is, until somehow we're brought face to face with the specter of death.

When we refuse to have a heart for the God who commands us to forgive, then we're open targets for Satan's schemes.

Lord, Give Me a Heart for You (2001)

God loves you unconditionally, Beloved. The question is: Do you love Him unconditionally?

Only you will ever limit what you are for God.

Beloved (1994)

You have been created by God and for God, and someday you will stand amazed at the simple yet profound ways He has used you even when you weren't aware of it.

No matter what happens, beloved, no matter how disappointing it is, you must, in an act of the will, rejoice and pray and give thanks.

As Silver Refined (1998)

Because of covenant, wounds need not leave scars. They can become imprints for the expression of His grace if only you will take God at His word—a word that cannot be broken and that will never be changed.

We need to simply do what we were created to do: love the Lord our God, obey His voice, hold fast to Him.

Our Covenant God (1999)

You will understand what God wants you to understand. He will teach you a little bit, and when you understand that, He will teach you a little bit more. The more you continue to study His Word, the more you will see and understand.

When you truly believe what the Bible says about Jesus Christ and decide to follow Him, to let Him be your Master, something miraculous happens.

God, Are You There? (1994)

Faith recognizes that God is in control, not man. Faith does it God's way, in God's timing—according to His good pleasure. Faith does not take life into its own hands, but in respect and trust places it in God's.

You can rest in the knowledge that even when bad things happen, God is always there. He is always in charge. Although He may not always deliver in the way you expect, you will find His grace sufficient.

When Bad Things Happen (2002)

Turn your heart's desire into a prayer. Tell your Father what you need. Thank Him that He wants to be known by you in greater depth!

Your life is to be lived in such a way as to reflect Him, to show the world the character of God—His love, His peace, His mercy, His gentleness. You are to live for Him, to accomplish His will. To miss this purpose is to miss fulfillment. It is to have existed rather than to have lived.

Lord, I Want to Know You (2000)

Real Christian life—the genuine article—is never hypocritical. Authentic Christian life is something higher, brighter, and infinitely more powerful than pale, phony substitutes.

How do you become poor in spirit? I believe it begins with catching a glimpse of God.

Lord, Only You Can Change Me (1995)

As human beings, hurts and wounds, bumps and bruises, disappointments and sorrows come bundled along with our birth certificates.

Man wants to think *he's* in charge, and that he has the first and last word about everything. But it isn't true. That sort of man-centered thinking has brought us into a world of hurt—literally!

When the Hurt Runs Deep: Healing and Hope for Life's Desperate Moments (2010)

A Christian marriage based on the precepts of God's Word can become a mini-culture of its own that refuses to be conformed to the larger culture. It resists being assimilated or swallowed up by the darkness, no matter how great and prevailing that darkness may be.

What is God's standard of success? It is obedience to His Word.

A Marriage without Regrets (2000)

I believe any child of God can be healed of the deepest, most horrendous wounds if he will learn three things: how to apply the balm of Gilead, how to follow the Great Physician's instructions, and how to give His medicine time to work.

When people do not listen to the Word of the Lord, it affects families, which in turn affect societies, which in turn affect nations, which in turn can affect the world.

Lord, Heal My Hurts (1989)

AUGUSTINE

Augustine is considered to be one of the most influential thinkers in the history of the church. His writings contributed greatly to the development of the church in Western Europe after the fall of the Roman Empire. Some contemporaries credit him with actually revitalizing the faith after Rome fell.

A Trinitarian, he also helped develop the doctrine of original sin. His teachings on salvation and divine grace have led to his being considered important to both the Catholic and Protestant churches.

He was born in AD 354 in Thagaste, Numidia (modern-day Algeria) and died in 430 in Hippo Regius, Numidia.

Augustine was the author of more than one hundred (surviving) written works, including *City of God*, *On Christian Doctrine*, *On the Trinity*, *On Free Choice of the Will*, and *Confessions*.

✍

Who can describe the tokens of God's goodness that are extended to the human race even in this life?

No man acts rightly save by the assistance of divine aid; and no man or devil acts unrighteously save by the permission of the divine and most just judgment.

It is true that wicked men do many things contrary to God's will; but so great is His wisdom and power, that all things which seem adverse to His purpose do still tend towards those just and good ends and issues which He Himself has foreknown.

Men are punished by God for their sins often visibly, always secretly, either in this life or after death.

It is He who gave to this intellectual nature free-will of such a kind, that if he wished to forsake God his blessedness, misery should forthwith result.

Why is it that we remember with difficulty, and without difficulty forget? Learn with difficulty, and without difficulty remain ignorant?

God is always trying to give good things to us, but our hands are too full to receive them.

There are wolves within, and there are sheep without.

I don't care to inquire why they cannot believe an earthly body can be in heaven, while the whole earth is suspended on nothing.

When men cannot communicate their thoughts to each other, simply because of difference of language, all the similarity of their common human nature is of no avail to unite them in fellowship.

His knowledge is not like ours, which has three tenses: present, past, and future. God's knowledge has no change or variation.

What grace is meant to do is to help good people, not to escape their sufferings, but to bear them with a stout heart, with a fortitude that finds its strength in faith.

For what is the self-complacent man but a slave to his own self-praise.

Since divine truth and scripture clearly teach us that God, the Creator of all things, is Wisdom, a true philosopher will be a lover of God. That does not mean that all who answer to the name are really in love with genuine wisdom, for it is one thing to be and another to be called a philosopher.

To love one's own self is nothing but to wish to be happy, and the standard is union with God. When, therefore, a person who knows how to love himself is bidden to love his neighbor as himself, is he not, in effect, commanded to persuade others, as far as he can, to love God?

It is no less impossible for us not to taste as bitter the death of those whose life for us was such a source of sweetness.

Sin is to a nature what blindness is to an eye. The blindness is an evil or defect which is a witness to the fact that the eye was created to see the light and, hence, the very lack of sight is the proof that the eye was meant. . .to be the one particularly capable of seeing the light. Were it not for this capacity, there would be no reason to think of blindness as a misfortune.

The bodies of irrational animals are bent toward the ground, whereas man was made to walk erect with his eyes on heaven, as though to remind him to keep his thoughts on things above.

For a prohibition always increases an illicit desire so long as the love of and joy in holiness is too weak to conquer the inclination to sin.

Pride is the beginning of sin. And what is pride but the craving for undue exaltation? And this is undue exaltation—when the soul abandons Him to whom it ought to cleave as its end, and becomes a kind of end to itself.

Though exposed to the same anguish, virtue and vice are not the same thing. For as the same fire causes gold to glow brightly, and chaff to smoke; and under the same flail the straw is beaten small, while the grain is cleansed; and as the lees are not mixed with the oil, though squeezed out of the vat by the same pressure, so the same violence of affliction proves, purges, clarifies the good, but damns, ruins, exterminates the wicked.

This joy in God is not like any pleasure found in physical or intellectual satisfaction. Nor is it such as a friend experiences in the presence of a friend. But, if we are to use any such analogy, it is more like the eye rejoicing in light.

In this present time we learn to bear with equanimity the ills to which even good men are subject, and to hold cheap the blessings which even the wicked enjoy.

The City of God (c. 410)

For Grace is given not because we have done good works, but in order that we may be able to do them.

Of the Spirit and the Letter (5th century)

Thou hast made us for Thyself, O Lord, and our heart is restless until it finds its rest in Thee.

And men go abroad to admire the heights of mountains, the mighty waves of the sea, the broad tides of rivers, the compass of the ocean, and the circuits of the stars, yet pass over the mystery of themselves without a thought.

How can the past and future be, when the past no longer is, and the future is not yet? As for the present, if it were always present and never moved on to become the past, it would not be time, but eternity.

The punishment of every disordered mind is its own disorder.

You never go away from us, yet we have difficulty in returning to You. Come, Lord, stir us up and call us back. Kindle and seize us. Be our fire and our sweetness. Let us love. Let us run.

The Bible was composed in such a way that as beginners mature, its meaning grows with them.

I was in misery, and misery is the state of every soul overcome by friendship with mortal things and lacerated when they are lost. Then the soul becomes aware of the misery which is its actual condition even before it loses them.

Late have I loved You, Beauty so old and so new: late have I loved You. And see, You were within and I was in the external world and sought You there, and in my unlovely state I plunged into those lovely created things which You made. You were with me, and I was not with You. The lovely things kept me far from You, though if they did not have their existence in You, they had no existence at all. You called and cried out loud and shattered my deafness. You were radiant and resplendent, You put to flight my blindness. You were fragrant, and I drew in my breath and now pant after You. I tasted You, and I feel but hunger and thirst for You. You touched me, and I am set on fire to attain the peace which is Yours.

For what am I to myself without You, but a guide to my own downfall?

No one knows what he himself is made of, except his own spirit within him, yet there is still some part of him which remains hidden even from his own spirit; but You, Lord, know everything about a human being because You have made him. . . . Let me, then, confess what I know about myself, and confess too what I do not know, because what I know of myself I know only because You shed light on me, and what I do not know I shall remain ignorant about until my darkness becomes like bright noon before Your face.

You are my Lord, because You have no need of my goodness.

Give me Yourself, O my God, give Yourself back to me. Lo, I love You, but if my love is too mean, let me love more passionately. I cannot gauge my love, nor know how far it fails, how much more love I need for my life to set its course straight into your arms, never swerving until hidden in the covert of your face. This alone I know, that without You all to me is misery, woe outside myself and woe within, and all wealth but penury, if it is not my God.

For you [God] are infinite and never change. In You "today" never comes to an end: and yet our "today" does come to an end in You, because time, as well as everything else, exists in You. If it did not, it would have no means of passing. And since Your years never come to an end, for You they are simply "today." . . . But You Yourself are eternally the same. In Your "today" You will make all that is to exist tomorrow and thereafter, and in Your "today" You have made all that existed yesterday and forever before.

What do I love when I love my God?

Your best servant is the person who does not attend so much to hearing what he himself wants as to willing what he has heard from You.

The mind commands the body and is instantly obeyed. The mind commands itself and meets resistance. The mind commands the hand to move, and it is so easy that one hardly distinguishes the order from its execution. Yet mind is mind and hand is body. The mind orders the mind to will. The recipient of the order is itself, yet it does not perform it.

For great are You, Lord, and You look kindly on what is humble, but the lofty-minded You regard from afar. Only to those whose hearts are crushed do You draw close. You will not let Yourself be found by the proud, nor even by those who in their inquisitive skill count stars or grains of sand, or measure the expanses of heaven, or trace the paths of the planets.

I look forward, not to what lies ahead of me in this life and will surely pass away, but to my eternal goal. I am intent upon this one purpose, not distracted by other aims, and with this goal in view I press on, eager for the prize, God's heavenly summons. Then I shall listen to the sound of Your praises and gaze at Your beauty ever present, never future, never past. But now my years are but sighs. You, O Lord, are my only solace. You, my Father, are eternal. But I am divided between time gone by and time to come, and its course is a mystery to me. My thoughts, the intimate life of my soul, are torn this way and that in the havoc of change. And so it will be until I am purified and melted by the fire of Your love and fused into one with You.

O Lord my God, tell me what you are to me. Say to my soul, *I am your salvation*. Say it so that I can hear it. My heart is listening, Lord; open the ears of my heart and say to my soul, *I am your salvation*. Let me run toward this voice and seize hold of You. Do not hide Your face from me: let me die so that I may see it, for not to see it would be death to me indeed.

How high a price we pay for the burden of habit! I am fitted for life here where I do not want to be, I want to live there but am unfit for it, and on both counts I am miserable.

Every day my conscience makes confession relying on the hope of Your mercy as more to be trusted than its own innocence.

Do they desire to join me in thanksgiving when they hear how, by Your gift, I have come close to You, and do they pray for me when they hear how I am held back by my own weight? . . . . A brotherly mind will love in me what You teach to be lovable, and will regret in me what You teach to be regrettable. This is a mark of a Christian brother's mind, not an outsider's.

A brotherly person rejoices on my account when he approves me, but when he disapproves, he is loving me. To such people I will reveal myself. They will take heart from my good traits, and sigh with sadness at my bad ones. My good points are instilled by You and are Your gifts. My bad points are my faults and Your judgments on them. Let them take heart from the one and regret the other. Let both praise and tears ascend in Your sight from brotherly hearts, Your censers. . . . . But You, Lord. . .make perfect my imperfections.

Often the contempt of vainglory becomes a source of even more vainglory, for it is not being scorned when the contempt is something one is proud of.

When I come to be united to Thee with all my being, then there will be no more pain and toil for me, and my life shall be a real life, being wholly filled by Thee.

The soul is torn apart in a painful condition as long as it prefers the eternal because of its Truth but does not discard the temporal because of familiarity.

To what place can I invite You, then, since I am in You? Or where could You come from, in order to come into me? To what place outside heaven and earth could I travel, so that my God could come to me there, the God who said, *I fill heaven and Earth*?

I inquired what wickedness is, and I didn't find a substance, but a perversity of will twisted away from the highest substance—You, O God—towards inferior things, rejecting its own inner life and swelling with external matter.

Someone who knows enough to become the owner of a tree, and gives thanks to You for the benefits it brings him, is in a better state, even if ignorant of its height in feet and the extent of its spread, than another who measures and counts all its branches but neither owns it nor knows its Creator nor loves Him.

The happy life is this—to rejoice to Thee, in Thee, and for Thee.

You are not the mind itself. For You are the Lord God of the mind. All these things are liable to change, but You remain immutable above all things.

Man, but a particle of Thy creation. . .

Confessions of St. Augustine (c. AD 397)

Richard Baxter, born in Rowton, England, in 1615, was at court to welcome the restoration of King Charles II to the British throne in the mid-seventeenth century. He was offered a royal chaplaincy but refused it because of his own Puritan leanings. He knew troubled times were coming, as Puritanism and Presbyterianism were falling out of favor.

When the Act of Conformity was passed into British Law, demanding allegiance to a common form of prayer, Baxter refused to conform and was jailed for a short time for his stance. He remained influential in "nonconformist" circles and was a prodigious writer on theological matters. He became known as "the chief of English Protestant Schoolmen" and died in London in 1691.

His written works include *The Reformed Pastor*, *The Saints' Everlasting Rest*, and a biography of his wife, Margaret, so the world would know of her virtues and tenderness.

✍

'Tis hard preaching a stone into tears, or making a rock to tremble.

We tell men what Christ hath done and suffered for their souls, and it scarce moves them.

The heart is naturally hard, and grows harder by custom in sin, especially by long abuse of mercy, neglect of the means of grace, and resisting the spirit of grace.

It is true, that men may have Christ whenever they are willing to comply with His terms. But if you are not willing now, how can you think you shall be willing hereafter?

Till men are deeply humbled, they can part with Christ and Salvation for a lust, for a little worldly gain, for that which is less than nothing. But when God hath enlightened their consciences, and broken their hearts, then they would give a world for Christ.

We can make them hear, but cannot make them feel. Our words stop in the porch of their ears and fancies, but enter not into their inward parts.

It is the case of most sinners to think themselves freest from those sins to which they are most enslaved.

What we most value, we shall think no pains too great to obtain.

The devils never had a Savior offered to them, but you have; and do you yet make light of Him?

When God hath shaken your careless soul out of your body, and you must answer for all your sins in your own name; O then, what would you give for a Savior!

The Causes and Danger of Slighting Christ and His Gospel (c. 1645)

Men would sooner believe that the gospel is from heaven, if they saw more such effects of it upon the hearts and lives of those who profess it.

He cannot succeed in healing the wounds of others who is himself unhealed by reason of neglecting himself.

For some persons there are who, though expert in spiritual ministry, go about it in a headstrong manner, and while acting intelligently, tread underfoot any good they do.

O sirs, it is a miserable thing when men study and talk of heaven and hell, and the fewness of the saved, and the difficulty of salvation, and be not all the while in good earnest.

Every man must render to God the things that are God's, and that, let it be remembered, is all he is and all he possesses.

We too easily play with the serpent's baits, and are ensnared by his wiles.

When we have led them to the living waters, if we muddy it by our filthy lives, we may lose our labor, and they be never the better.

One word of seasonable, prudent advice, given by a minister to persons in necessity, may be of more use than many sermons.

The world is better able to read the nature of religion in a man's life than in the Bible.

Even the stoutest sinners will hear us on their death-bed, though they scorned us before.

The Reformed Pastor (c. 1645)

What if God withdraw His patience and sustenation, and let you drop into hell while you are quarrelling with His Word?—Will you then believe that there is no hell?

If you will believe God, believe this: there is but one of these two ways for every wicked man, either conversion or damnation.

You are but dead and damned men, except you will be converted. Should I tell you otherwise, I should deceive you with a lie.

The law was not made for you to judge, but that you might be ruled and judged by it.

It is the unchangeable law of God, that wicked men must turn or die.

It hath been the astonishing wonder of many a man, as well as me, to read in the holy scripture, how few will be saved.

If sin be such an evil that it requires the death of Christ for its expiation, no wonder if it deserve our everlasting misery.

Few men are apt to believe that which they would not have to be true, and fewer would have that to be true, which they apprehend to be against them.

As the fire doth mount upwards, and the needle that is touched with the lodestone still turneth to the north, so the converted soul is inclined to God.

A Call to the Unconverted, to Turn and Live (c. 1640)

BERNARD OF CLAIRVAUX

Bernard, a son of French nobility, was born in 1090 in Fontaine les Dijon, France. At the age of nineteen he joined the Benedictine monastery at Citeaux. Three years later he was sent to found a new abbey, which he named Claire Vallée. That name evolved into Clairvaux, the name by which he is known to history.

With the death of Pope Honorius II in 1130, a major schism occurred in the church. Bernard traveled across Europe convincing many powerful lords and kings to renew their allegiance. In doing so he may have saved the Catholic Church.

He was also a founding member of the Cistercian Order, and he outlined the policies that would come to govern the Knights Templar. Later one of his own pupils would become pope. He died in 1153 in Clairvaux.

His written works include *The Steps of Humility and Pride*, *On Grace and Free Choice*, and *In Praise of the New Knighthood*.

✍

Many of those who are humiliated are not humble. Some react to humiliation with anger, others with patience, and others with freedom. The first are culpable, the next harmless, the last just.

On the Song of Songs I (12th century)

If you concentrate hard on the state you are in, it would be surprising if you have time for anything else.

Selected Works (12th century)

Vines and trees will teach you that which you will never learn from masters.

Honey and Salt: Selected Spiritual Writings (12th century)

You want me to tell you why God is to be loved and how much. I answer, the reason for loving God is God Himself; and the measure of love due to Him is immeasurable love.

Perfect love of God with our heart, soul, mind, and strength will not happen until we are no longer compelled to think about ourselves.

Just as air flooded with the light of the sun is transformed into the same splendor of the light so that it appears to be light itself, so it is like for those who melt away from themselves and are entirely transfused into the will of God.

We are to love God for Himself, because of a twofold reason; nothing is more reasonable, nothing more profitable. When one asks, Why should I love God? he may mean, What is lovely in God? or What shall I gain by loving God? In either case, the same sufficient cause of love exists, namely, God Himself.

Could any title be greater than this, that He gave Himself for us unworthy wretches? And being God, what better gift could He offer than Himself? Hence, if one seeks for God's claim upon our love here is the chiefest: Because He first loved us (1 John 4:19).

Ought He not to be loved in return, when we think who loved, whom He loved, and how much He loved?

Whosoever praises God for His essential goodness, and not merely because of the benefits He has bestowed, does really love God for God's sake, and not selfishly.

On Loving God (12th century)

BLACKABY, HENRY

Henry Blackaby was born in British Columbia, Canada, in 1935. Since 1970, when he became pastor of a small church in Saskatoon, Henry Blackaby's life has been spent in ministry. He has been a music director, education director, and pastor in churches in the United States and Canada. He was president of both the Canadian Baptist Theological College and the Canadian Southern Baptist Conference.

Henry and his wife, Marylinn, set up Blackaby Ministries International to help people, churches, leaders, and families either return to God or strengthen their relationship with Him. All five of the Blackabys' children play active roles in the organization.

His books include *Experiencing God: Knowing and Doing the Will of God*, *Experiencing God Together*, and *Experiencing God Day by Day: A Devotional*.

All Christians are called to develop God-given talents, to make the most of their lives, to develop to the fullest their God-given powers and capacities.

Spiritual Leadership (2001)

Christianity is not merely a religion; it is a relationship with a Person.

Watch to see where God is working and join Him!

Experiencing God (2007)

When we hear His call and respond appropriately, there will be no limit to what God can and will do through His people. But if we do not even recognize when He is speaking, we are in trouble at the very heart of our relationship to Him.

Regardless of what we say, it's what we do that reveals what we as a church or individual actually believe about God and His will for us.

What the Spirit Is Saying to the Churches (2003)

Will God ever ask you to do something you are not able to do? The answer is yes—all the time! It must be that way, for God's glory and kingdom.

If we function according to our ability alone, we get the glory; if we function according to the power of the Spirit within us, God gets the glory. He wants to reveal Himself to a watching world.

Experiencing the Spirit: The Power of Pentecost Every Day (2009)

People who make decisions based merely on what seems most advisable to them will inevitably choose something inferior to God's best.

Jesus, the ultimate model for the Christian life, did not rely on His own best thinking, but depended completely on His heavenly Father for wisdom in everything.

Hearing God's Voice (2002)

Two things are involved in taking the ordinary and making it extraordinary: a man and almighty God in a covenant relationship. We are the ordinary. The extraordinary comes from God's nature.

The good news is that God changes the hearts of men.

The Man God Uses (with Tom Blackaby, 1999)

The message of the early church, as told in the book of Acts, is that the bare simplicity of the Christian faith is what counts. The testimony of these early Christians was that of God's people proclaiming the gospel in the power of the Holy Spirit. . .and confirming it with holy lives.

What's So Spiritual about Your Gifts? (with Mel Blackaby, 2004)

Revival quickens the human spirit and enlivens worship. It makes prayer exciting, preaching dynamic, and Christian service fervent.

Revival amplifies the Christian experience, making the Holy Spirit's work in a person's life unmistakable.

Fresh Encounter (with Richard Blackaby, 2009)

When we look at the people God used in the scriptures as well as those He used throughout Christian history, we see their lives marked by a deep awareness and practice of prayer with their heavenly Father.

Every part of our Lord's life was centered and guided by His continuing communication with the Father.

Experiencing Prayer with Jesus (with Norman Blackaby, 2006)

Too many of God's people are going through life missing most of what their Father in heaven intends for them to experience, and an inadequate grasp of the cross lies at the heart of this tragedy.

How serious is sin? Serious enough that to provide a way to deal with it, God the Father ordained the death of His own beloved Son, a death far more profound than physical death.

Experiencing the Cross (2005)

It is clear that God desires to give you wisdom and show you His purpose for your life. Be prepared to receive all that God teaches you through the Holy Spirit.

The deepest longing in a person's heart is to have a relationship with God.

A God-Centered Church: Experiencing God Together
(with Melvin Blackaby, 2007)

God still uses people today for His purposes and for His glory.

God continues to work through those who are willing to pay the necessary price to walk with Him.

Called to Be God's Leader (with Richard Blackaby, 2004)

The ways of God are wonderful and mysterious!

The Bible is the record of God! It reveals His nature and His ways in the midst of His people.

Created to Be God's Friend (1999)

BOUNDS, E. M.

Born in 1835 in Shelbyville, Missouri, Edward McKendree Bounds was the son of a Missouri settler. After his father died, he joined the westward trek to California, but finding no gold there, he returned to Missouri and trained as a lawyer.

After meeting the evangelist Smith Thomas, he enrolled in Centenary Seminary. At the age of twenty-four he became pastor of Monticello Methodist Church in Palmyra, Missouri.

Despite being opposed to slavery, he was arrested and jailed by Unionist forces during the Civil War. On his release he became chaplain to the Confederate Army.

E. M. Bounds died in 1913 in Washington, Georgia. Only two of his books were published during his lifetime, but admirers were unwilling to let that situation stand and saw to it that many more books and compilations were published.

His written works include *Power through Prayer*; *Prayer and Praying Men*; *Satan: His Personality, Power, and Overthrow*; and *Heaven: A Place, a City, a Home*.

Faith brings great ease of mind and perfect peace of heart.

True prayers are born of present trials and present needs.

Daily prayer for daily needs.

Faith thrives in an atmosphere of prayer.

Faith starts prayer to work—clears the way to the mercy seat.

He prays not at all, who does not press his plea.

Conduct is what we do, character is what we are.

Character is the root of the tree, conduct, the fruit it bears.

Delay is often the test and the strength of Faith.

Faith gathers strength by waiting and praying.

Faith grows by reading and meditating upon the Word of God.

Patience has its perfect work in the school of delay.

Bread for today is bread enough.

We must trust God today, and leave tomorrow with him.

Trust always operates in the present tense.

Faith deals with God, and is conscious of God.

Faith is not believing just anything; it is believing God.

The present is ours; the future belongs to God.

The Necessity of Prayer (late 19th century)

The church is looking for better methods; God is looking for better men.

The glory and efficiency of the gospel are staked on the men who proclaim it.

The gospel of Christ does not move by popular waves.

The Holy Spirit does not flow through methods but through men.

The character as well as the fortunes of the gospel are committed to the preacher. He makes or mars the message from God to man.

Prayer is the preacher's mightiest weapon.

The sermon cannot rise in its life-giving forces above the man. Dead men give out dead sermons and dead sermons kill. Everything depends on the spiritual character of the preacher.

The sweetest graces by a slight perversion may bear the bitterest fruit.

Truth unquickened by God's Spirit deadens as much as, or more than, error.

The preacher's strongest and sharpest preaching should be to himself.

Power through Prayer (1906)

Without devotion prayer is an empty form.

The spirit of devotion puts God in all things.

Humility retires itself from the public gaze.

Humility never exalts itself.

Humility is an indispensable requisite of true prayer.

Humility must be in the praying character as light is in the sun.

Kneeling well becomes us as the attitude of prayer, because it betokens humility.

The Essentials of Prayer (late 19th century)

BROTHER LAWRENCE

Born in Herimenil, France, in 1611, Nicholas Herman was a soldier during a portion of the Thirty Years War. At age twenty-four he retreated from the world by joining the Carmelite Monastery in Paris, where he became known as Brother Lawrence of the Resurrection.

Lacking the education required to become a cleric, he became a lay brother. In addition to his religious duties, his main responsibilities were kitchen work and the repairing of the monks' leather sandals.

His piety and his habitual practice of raising even the most menial of tasks as offerings to God eventually garnered him some attention. But it wasn't until long after his death in 1691 that he became well known outside the religious community in Paris, when his correspondence with a local priest was compiled and published under the title *The Practice of the Presence of God*.

Good when He gives, supremely good;
    Nor less when He denies:
Afflictions, from His sovereign hand,
    Are blessings in disguise.

Have courage then: make a virtue of necessity: ask of God, not deliverance from your pains, but strength to bear resolutely, for the love of Him, all that He should please, and as long as He shall please.

We cannot have too much in so good and faithful a Friend, who will never fail us in this world nor in the next.

Our only business is to love and delight ourselves in God.

Let us thus think often that our only business in this life is to please God, that perhaps all besides is but folly and vanity.

In order to form a habit of conversing with God continually, and referring all we do to Him; we must at first apply to Him with some diligence: but that after a little care we should find His love inwardly excite us to it without any difficulty.

We ought to act with God in the greatest simplicity, speaking to Him frankly and plainly, and imploring His assistance in our affairs, just as they happen.

We need only to recognize God intimately present with us, to address ourselves to Him every moment.

There is not in the world a kind of life more sweet and delightful than that of a continual conversation with God.

That there needed neither art nor science for going to God, but only a heart resolutely determined to apply itself to nothing but Him, or for His sake, and to love Him only.

I renounced, for the love of Him, everything that was not He; and I began to live as if there was none but He and I in the world.

Do not always scrupulously confine yourself to certain rules, or particular forms of devotion; but act with a general confidence in God, with love and humility.

Let all our employment be to know God: the more one knows Him, the more one desires to know Him.

In difficulties we need only have recourse to Jesus Christ, and beg His grace, with which everything became easy.

Having resolved to make the love of God the end of all his actions, he had found reasons to be well satisfied with his method.

The greatest glory we can give to God is to distrust our own strength utterly, and to commit ourselves wholly to His safe-keeping.

We have a God who is infinitely gracious, and knows all our wants.

I considered myself before Him as a poor criminal at the feet of his judge; at other times I beheld Him in my heart as my Father.

I hope that when I have done what I can, He will do with me what He pleases.

I have no pain or difficulty about my state, because I have no will but that of God, which I endeavor to accomplish in all things.

Blind as we are, we hinder God, and stop the current of His graces. But when He finds a soul penetrated with a lively faith, He pours into it His graces and favors plentifully.

We know also that we can do all things with the grace of God, which He never refuses to them who ask it earnestly.

We should feed and nourish our souls with high notions of God; which would yield us great joy in being devoted to Him.

I wish you could convince yourself that God is often (in some sense) nearer to us and more effectually present with us, in sickness than in health.

So that if in this life we would enjoy the peace of paradise, we must accustom ourselves to a familiar, humble, affectionate conversation with Him.

But those who have the gale of the Holy Spirit go forward even in sleep.

When unadorned, adorned the most.

Are we not rude and deserve blame, if we leave Him alone, to busy ourselves about trifles, which do not please Him and perhaps offend Him? 'Tis to be feared these trifles will one day cost us dear.

It matters not to me what I do, or what I suffer, so long as I abide lovingly united to God's will—that is my whole business.

The loss of a friend may lead to acquaintance with the Friend.

This King, full of mercy and goodness, very far from chastising me, embraces me with love, makes me eat at His table, serves me with His own hands, gives me the key of His treasures.

He converses and delights Himself with me incessantly, in a thousand and a thousand ways, and treats me in all respects as His favorite.

If we knew how much He loves us, we should be always ready to receive equally and with indifference from His hand the sweet and the bitter; all would please that came from Him.

We ought not to be weary of doing little things for the love of God, who regards not the greatness of the work, but the love with which it is performed.

I shall have this good at least; that till death I shall have done all that is in me to love Him.

I am filled with shame and confusion, when I reflect on the one hand upon the great favors which God has done, and incessantly continues to do, me; and on the other, upon the ill use I have made of them, and my small advancement in the way of perfection. His prayer was nothing else but a sense of the presence of God.

When the appointed times of prayer were past, he found no difference, because he still continued with God, praising and blessing Him with all his might, so that he passed his life in continual joy.

A little lifting up the heart suffices; a little remembrance of God, one act of inward worship, though upon a march, and sword in hand, are prayers which however short, are nevertheless very acceptable to God.

The least little remembrance will always be acceptable to Him. You need not cry very loud.

He is always near you and with you; leave Him not alone.

Let us fear to leave Him. Let us be always with Him. Let us live and die in His presence.

The whole substance of religion was faith, hope, and charity; by the practice of which we become united to the will of God.

I did not engage in a religious life but for the love of God, and I have endeavored to act only for Him; whatever becomes of me, whether I be lost or saved.

God seemed to have granted the greatest favors to the greatest sinners, as more signal monuments of His mercy.

If the vessel of our soul is still tossed with winds and storms, let us awake the Lord, who reposes in it, and He will quickly calm the sea.

Love sweetens pain; and when one loves God, one suffers for His sake with joy and courage.

When I fail in my duty, I readily acknowledge it, saying, I am used to do so: I shall never do otherwise, if I am left to myself. If I fail not, then I give God thanks, acknowledging that it comes from Him.

He requires no great matters of us; a little remembrance of Him from time to time, a little adoration: sometimes to pray for His grace, sometimes to offer

Him your sufferings, and sometimes to return Him thanks for the favors He has given you.

I do not pray that you may be delivered from your pains, but I pray God earnestly that He would give you strength and patience to bear them as long as He pleases.

The trust we put in God honors Him much, and draws down great graces.

As he proceeded in his work, he continued his familiar conversation with his Maker, imploring His grace, and offering to Him all his actions.

The end we ought to propose to ourselves is to become, in this life, the most perfect worshippers of God we can possibly be, as we hope to be through all eternity.

The Practice of the Presence of God (17th century)

BUECHNER, FREDERICK

Carl Frederick Buechner was born in 1926 in New York City. An ordained Presbyterian minister, he has also had a writing career that spans six decades. The *New York Times* called him "a major talent." His writing has won many awards, and he is consistently listed as one of the most read authors among Christian readers.

When he became a Presbyterian minister, many who knew him were surprised, and some thought the world might have lost a great novelist in exchange for a mediocre preacher. But the preaching seems to have fed the writing and the writing inspired the preaching. Both have gone from strength to strength. His writing style encourages readers to see grace in the everyday aspects of ordinary lives.

His books include *A Long Day's Dying*, *The Magnificent Defeat*, *The Hungering Dark*, *Faces of Jesus*, and *The Book of Bebb*.

Compassion is. . .the sometimes-fatal capacity for feeling what it's like to live inside somebody else's skin.

To confess your sins to God is not to tell God anything God doesn't already know. Until you confess them, however, they are the abyss between you. When you confess them, they become the Golden Gate Bridge.

Beyond Words: Daily Readings in the ABCs of Faith (2004)

The preaching of the gospel is a telling of the truth or the putting of a sort of frame of words around the silence that is truth because truth in the sense of fullness, of the way things are, can at best be only pointed to by the language of poetry—of metaphor, image, symbol—as it is used in the Prophets of the Old Testament and elsewhere.

Telling the Truth: The Gospel as Tragedy, Comedy, and Fairy Tale (1977)

It is as impossible for man to demonstrate the existence of God as it would be for even Sherlock Holmes to demonstrate the existence of Arthur Conan Doyle.

The place God calls you to is the place where your deep gladness and the world's deep hunger meet.

Wishful Thinking: A Seeker's ABC

Listen to your life. See it for the fathomless mystery it is. In the boredom and pain of it, no less than in the excitement and gladness: touch, taste, smell your way to the holy and hidden heart of it, because in the last analysis all moments are key moments, and life itself is grace.

Now and Then: A Memoir of Vocation

Life is grace. Sleep is forgiveness. The night absolves. Darkness wipes the slate clean, not spotless to be sure, but clean enough for another day's chalking.

A miracle is when the whole is greater than the sum of its parts. A miracle is when one plus one equals a thousand.

The Alphabet of Grace (2009)

Stop trying to protect, to rescue, to judge, to manage the lives around you.
. . . Remember that the lives of others are not your business. They are their
business. They are God's business. . . . Even your own life is not your business.
It also is God's business. Leave it to God.

What we hunger for perhaps more than anything else is to be known in our
full humanness, and yet that is often just what we also fear more than anything else. It is important to tell at least from time to time the secret of who
we truly and fully are . . .because otherwise we run the risk of losing track of
who we truly and fully are and little by little come to accept instead the highly
edited version which we put forth in hope that the world will find it more
acceptable than the real thing. It is important to tell our secrets too because
it makes it easier. . .for other people to tell us a secret or two of their own.

Telling Secrets (2000)

If we are to love our neighbors, before doing anything else we must see our
neighbors. With our imagination as well as our eyes, that is to say like artists,
we must see not just their faces but the life behind and within their faces.
Here it is love that is the frame we see them in.

Whistling in the Dark: A Doubter's Dictionary (1993)

To be commanded to love God at all, let alone in the wilderness, is like being
commanded to be well when we are sick, to sing for joy when we are dying of
thirst, to run when our legs are broken. But this is the first and great commandment nonetheless. Even in the wilderness—especially in the wilderness—you
shall love Him.

A Room Called Remember: Uncollected Pieces (1992)

Much as we wish, not one of us can bring back yesterday or shape tomorrow.
Only today is ours, and it will not be ours for long, and once it is gone it will
never in all time be ours again. Thou only knowest what it holds in store for
us, yet even we know something of what it will hold. The chance to speak the
truth, to show mercy, to ease another's burden. The chance to resist evil, to
remember all the good times and good people of our past, to be brave, to be
strong, to be glad.

The life I touch for good or ill will touch another life, and in turn another, until who knows where the trembling stops or in what far place my touch will be felt.

The Hungering Dark (1985)

The love for equals is a human thing—of friend for friend, brother for brother. It is to love what is loving and lovely. The world smiles. The love for the less fortunate is a beautiful thing—the love for those who suffer, for those who are poor, the sick, the failures, the unlovely. This is compassion, and it touches the heart of the world. The love for the more fortunate is a rare thing—to love those who succeed where we fail, to rejoice without envy with those who rejoice, the love of the poor for the rich, of the black man for the white man. The world is always bewildered by its saints. And then there is the love for the enemy—love for the one who does not love you but mocks, threatens, and inflicts pain. The tortured's love for the torturer. This is God's love. It conquers the world.

For outlandish creatures like us, on our way to a heart, a brain, and courage, Bethlehem is not the end of our journey but only the beginning—not home but the place through which we must pass if ever we are to reach home at last.

The Magnificent Defeat (1985)

It's less the words they say than those they leave unsaid that split old friends apart.

Godric (1999)

To journey for the sake of saving our own lives is little by little to cease to live in any sense that really matters, even to ourselves, because it is only by journeying for the world's sake—even when the world bores and sickens and scares you half to death—that little by little we start to come alive.

Listen. Your life is happening. You are happening. Think back on your journey. The music of your life. . . .

The Sacred Journey: A Memoir of Early Days (1991)

Part of the inner world of everyone is this sense of emptiness, unease, incompleteness, and I believe that this in itself is a word from God, that this is the sound that God's voice makes in a world that has explained Him away. In such a world, I suspect that maybe God speaks to us most clearly through His silence, His absence, so that we know Him best through our missing Him.

Secrets in the Dark: A Life in Sermons (2007)

CALVIN, JOHN

John Calvin (or Jehan Cauvan) was born in Noyon, France, in 1509, where he trained as a lawyer. At the age of twenty-one, in the midst of the Protestant Revolution, he left the Catholic Church. When it became dangerous to be a Protestant in that country, he fled to Switzerland, where he worked on reforming the Swiss church and became pastor to a growing number of French refugees.

A major tenet of his teaching was that God alone determined (and had already determined) who would be saved and who would not. His writings and preaching became the foundations of the movement known as Calvinism and greatly influenced the Reformed, Congregational, and Presbyterian churches. He died in 1564 in Geneva, Switzerland.

His writings include *Institutes of the Christian Religion*, commentaries on the Bible, and *On Civil Authority*.

✍

Angels, being the ministers appointed to execute the commands of God, must, of course, be admitted to be His creatures, but to stir up questions concerning the time or order in which they were created bespeaks more perverseness than industry.

Though our eyes, in what direction soever they turn, are forced to behold the works of God, we see how fleeting our attention is, and holy quickly pious thoughts, if any arise, vanish away.

The most audacious despiser of God is most easily disturbed, trembling at the sound of a falling leaf.

When he chooses to worship wood and stone rather than be thought to have no God, it is evident how very strong this impression of a Deity must be; since it is more difficult to obliterate it from the mind of man, than to break down the feelings of his nature.

For how can the human mind which has not yet been able to ascertain of what the body of the sun consists, though it is daily presented to the eye, bring down the boundless essence of God to its little measure?

No man can survey himself without forthwith turning his thoughts towards the God in whom he lives and moves; because it is perfectly obvious, that the endowments which we possess cannot possibly be from ourselves; nay, that our very being is nothing else than subsistence in God alone.

That there exists in the human minds and indeed by natural instinct, some sense of Deity, we hold to be beyond dispute, since God Himself, to prevent any man from pretending ignorance, has endued all men with some idea of His Godhead, the memory of which He constantly renews and occasionally enlarges, that all to a man being aware that there is a God, and that He is their Maker, may be condemned by their own conscience when they neither worship Him nor consecrate their lives to His service.

But, as a heathen tells us, there is no nation so barbarous, no race so brutish, as not to be imbued with the conviction that there is a God.

Unless everything peculiar to divinity is confined to God alone, He is robbed of His honor, and His worship is violated.

Since we are all naturally prone to hypocrisy, any empty semblance of righteousness is quite enough to satisfy us instead of righteousness itself.

Since the Holy Spirit always instructs us in what is useful, but altogether omits, or only touches cursorily on matters which tend little to edification, of all such matters, it certainly is our duty to remain in willing ignorance.

Let us here remember that on the whole subject of religion one rule of modesty and soberness is to be observed, and it is this, in obscure matters not to speak or think, or even long to know, more than the Word of God has delivered.

Until men feel that they owe everything to God, that they are cherished by His paternal care, and that He is the author of all their blessings, so that nought is to be looked for away from Him, they will never submit to Him in voluntary obedience; nay, unless they place their entire happiness in Him, they will never yield up their whole selves to Him in truth and sincerity.

So long as we do not look beyond the earth, we are quite pleased with our own righteousness, wisdom, and virtue; we address ourselves in the most flattering terms, and seem only less than demigods.

Every person, on coming to the knowledge of himself, is not only urged to seek God, but is also led as by the hand to find Him.

The scriptures teach that there is essentially but one God, and, therefore, that the essence both of the Son and Spirit is unbegotten.

Our wisdom, in so far as it ought to be deemed true and solid Wisdom, consists almost entirely of two parts: the knowledge of God and of ourselves.

Since the Lord has been pleased to instruct us, not in frivolous questions, but in solid piety, in the fear of His name, in true faith, and the duties of holiness, let us rest satisfied with such knowledge.

Never to attempt to search after God anywhere but in His sacred word, and never to speak or think of Him farther than we have it for our guide.

In reading the scriptures we should constantly direct our inquiries and meditations to those things which tend to edification, not indulge in curiosity, or in studying things of no use.

Institutes of the Christian Religion (16th century)

There is wide difference between wise caution and perverse squeamishness.

We know what a strong propensity men have to falsehood, so that they not only have a natural desire to be deceived, but each individual appears to be ingenious in deceiving himself.

The flesh is willing to flatter itself, and many who now give themselves every indulgence, promise to themselves an easy entrance into life. Thus men practice mutual deception on each other and fall asleep in wicked indifference.

Satan, who is a wonderful contriver of delusions, is constantly laying snares to entrap ignorant and heedless persons.

If the aspect of the world now dazzles your eyes, the last day will cure you of this folly, but it will be too late.

We cannot rely on God's promises without obeying His commandments.

Bible Commentaries: Matthew, Mark, and Luke (mid-16th century)

CARMICHAEL, AMY

Amy Carmichael, born in Ireland in 1866, was the daughter of a pastor. When Amy was in her late teens, she began teaching a Sunday morning class for female mill workers in Belfast, Ireland. Later she carried on the same ministry in Manchester, England, where she attended a talk given by the missionary Hudson Taylor.

She determined to follow his example but was declared unfit on the day she was due to sail for China. Instead, she joined the Church Missionary Society, which eventually sent her to India. There she devoted the rest of her life to spreading the Gospel and saving children from lives of prostitution as temple servants. Her Dohnavur Fellowship in Tamil Nadu eventually housed a thousand children. She died in 1951 in Tamil Nadu.

Her written works include *Things as They Are: Mission Work in Southern India*, *Candles in the Dark*, and *Whispers of His Power*.

We are weaving for God the garment, the only garment, they may ever see by Him.

Will you not ask that we may be saved from ever, by word or look or gesture, pushing a soul back into the dark?

Oh is it not a magnificent thing to be privileged thus, in any small measure, to spread the glorious tidings of our blessed Lord!

What will you wish you had done, when the King comes?
He who wept over the city in olden time cares still, as He looks upon the sinning and the suffering of today.

From Sunrise Land: Letters from Japan (1895)

Love knows how to do without what it naturally wants. Love knows how to say, "What does it matter?"

It is not the place where we are, or the work that we do or cannot do, that matters, it is something else. It is the fire within that burns and shines, whatever be our circumstances.

Edges of His Ways (1955)

Do not fight the thing in detail: turn from it. Look *only* at your Lord. Sing. Read. Work.

Even though we must walk in the land of fear, there is no need to fear. The power of His resurrection comes before the fellowship of His sufferings.

Gold by Moonlight (1935)

The word *comfort* is from two Latin words meaning "with" and "strong"—He is with us to make us strong. Comfort is not soft, weakening commiseration; it is true, strengthening love.

Kohila: The Shaping of an Indian Nurse (1939)

If by doing some work which the undiscerning consider "not spiritual work" I can best help others, and I inwardly rebel, thinking it is the spiritual for which I crave, when in truth it is the interesting and exciting, then I know nothing of Calvary love.

If I am afraid to speak the truth lest I lose affection, or lest the one concerned should say, "You do not understand," or because I fear to lose my reputation for kindness; if I put my own good name before the other's highest good, then I know nothing of Calvary love.

If (1939)

Can we follow the Savior far, who have no wound or scar?

God hold us to that which drew us first, when the Cross was the attraction, and we wanted nothing else.

God's Missionary (1997)

All along, let us remember we are not asked to understand, but simply to obey.

A cup brimful of sweetness cannot spill even one drop of bitter water, no matter how suddenly jarred.

Candles in the Dark (1982)

As the needs of all living things must, we have proved that it is a very safe thing to trust in the Lord our God.

Gold Cord (1957)

CHAMBERS, OSWALD

Oswald Chambers was born in 1874 into a devout Baptist family in Aberdeen, Scotland. As a teenager his spirituality and work to evangelize the slum areas were already being noticed.

At the outbreak of World War I, he left his position as principal of the Clapham Common Bible Training College in England and joined the YMCA as a chaplain, where his responsibility was preaching to the troops.

Stricken with appendicitis while in Cairo, Egypt, he refused a hospital bed, insisting it could be better used by a wounded soldier. He died shortly afterwards, in 1917.

His sermons and other works were saved for posterity by his widow, Gertrude, who, as a partner in his ministry, had transcribed his sermons. Over thirty books would be produced from these notes.

His books include *Baffled to Fight Better* and *My Utmost for His Highest*, compiled by Gertrude.

God does not expect us to imitate Jesus Christ: He expects us to allow the life of Jesus to be manifested in our moral flesh.

The mere reading of the Word of God has power to communicate the life of God to us mentally, morally, and spiritually.

Approved unto God (1941)

Keep your life so constant in its contact with God that His surprising power may break out on the right hand and on the left. Always be in a state of expectancy, and see that you leave room for God to come in as He likes.

The aim of the missionary is to do God's will, not to be useful, not to win the heathen; he is useful and he does win the heathen, but that is not his aim. His aim is to do the will of his Lord.

My Utmost for His Highest (1935)

Only one in a thousand sits down in the midst of it all and says—I will watch my Father mend this. God must not be treated as a hospital for our broken "toys," but as our Father.

Not Knowing Where (1957)

The sympathy which is reverent with what it cannot understand is worth its weight in gold.

Baffled to Fight Better (1931)

There is something in human pride that can stand big troubles, but we need the supernatural grace and power of God to stand by us in the little things. The tiniest detail in which we obey has all the omnipotent power of the grace of God behind it. When we do our duty, not for duty's sake, but because we believe that God is engineering our circumstances in that way, then at the very point of our obedience the whole superb grace of God is ours.

Our Brilliant Heritage (1965)

The touchstone of the Holy Spirit's work in us is the answer to our Lord's question: "Who do men say that the Son of Man is?"

Our Lord makes human destiny depend on that one thing, who men say He is, because the revelation of who Jesus is is only given by the Holy Spirit.

Spiritual maturity is not reached by the passing of the years, but by obedience to the will of God.

Some people mature into an understanding of God's will more quickly than others because they obey more readily; they more readily sacrifice the life of nature to the will of God.

Bringing Sons into Glory and Making All Things New (1982)

The call of God is a call according to the nature of God; where we go in obedience to that call depends entirely on the providential circumstances which God engineers, and is not of any moment. The danger is to fit the call of God into the idea of our own discernment and say, "God called me there." If we say so and stick to it, then it is good-bye to the development of the life of God in us.

Psychology of Redemption (1922)

God is not preparing you for anything; obedience is its own end in the purpose of God; be faithful to Him.

We are apt to imagine that if Jesus Christ constrains us and we obey Him, He will lead us to great success; but He does not. If our Lord has ever constrained you, and you obeyed Him, what was your dream of His purpose? Never put your dream of success as God's purpose for you; His purpose may be exactly the opposite.

God's Workmanship / He Shall Glorify Me (1997)

Satan takes occasion of the frailty of the bodily temple and says, "Now you know you cannot do that; you are so infirm, you cannot concentrate your mind," etc. Never allow bodily infirmities to hinder your obeying the commands of Jesus.

If Thou Wilt Be Perfect (1963)

The test of mountain-top experiences, of mysticism, of visions of God and of solitariness is when you are "in the soup" of actual circumstances.

Shade of His Hand (1962)

Emotion is not simply an overplus of feeling; it is life lived at white-heat, a state of wonder. To lose wonder is to lose the true element of religion.

The Pilgrim's Songbook (1941)

The Bible attitude is not that God sends sickness or that sickness is of the devil, but that sickness is a fact usable by both God and the devil.

Philosophy of Sin (1960)

The sense of mystery must always be, for mystery means being guided by obedience to Someone who knows more than I do.

The Place of Help (1936)

God never estimates what we give from impulse. We are given credit for what we determine in our hearts to give; for the giving that is governed by a fixed determination. The Spirit of God revolutionizes our philanthropic instincts. Much of our philanthropy is simply the impulse to save ourselves an uncomfortable feeling. The Spirit of God alters all that. As saints our attitude towards giving is that we give for Jesus Christ's sake, and from no other motive.

Biblical Psychology: Christ-Centered Solutions for Daily Problems (1968)

Jesus did not stand as a prophet and utter judgments; wherever He went the unerring directness of His presence located men.

He Shall Glorify Me (1965)

We become side-tracked if we make physical health our aim and imagine that because we are children of God we shall always be perfectly well.

The Highest Good / The Shadow of an Agony (1992)

Consecration would soon be changed into sanctification if we would only concentrate on what God wants.

Studies in the Sermon on the Mount (1941)

CHESTERTON, G. K.

Born in London in 1874, Gilbert Keith Chesterton was a writer, lay theologian, Christian apologist, art critic. . .and many other things. His intellect and literary talents drew praise from both sides of the religious/rationalist debate.

His literary creation, the detective Father Brown, often saw solving crimes as secondary to redeeming those committing them.

A large man, prolific writer, and flamboyant dresser (often sporting a cape and carrying a sword-stick), Chesterton made a big impact on the English society of his time. When he died in 1936, it was suggested that a whole generation seemed to have grown up under his influence.

His books include *The Everlasting Man*, *Eugenics and Other Evils*, *Orthodoxy*, and the Father Brown stories.

✍

A man should not sacrifice what he does not esteem.

The Collected Works of G. K. Chesterton

The Christian idea has not been tried and found wanting. It has been found difficult and left untried.

The Homelessness of Man (1910)

Fallacies do not cease to be fallacies because they become fashions.

The Illustrated London News (1930)

The great misfortune of the modern English is not at all that they are more boastful than other people (they are not); it is that they are boastful about those particular things which nobody can boast of without losing them.

Men trust an ordinary man because they trust themselves. But men trust a great man because they do not trust themselves. And hence the worship of great men always appears in times of weakness and cowardice; we never hear of great men until the time when all other men are small.

All the absurd physical metaphors, such as youth and age, living and dying, are, when applied to nations, but pseudo-scientific attempts to conceal from men the awful liberty of their lonely souls.

America, of course, like every other human thing, can in a spiritual sense live or die as much as it chooses. But at the present moment the matter which America has very seriously to consider is not how near it is to its birth and beginning, but how near it may be to its end.

Democracy is not philanthropy; it is not even altruism or social reform. Democracy is not founded on pity for the common man; democracy is founded on reverence for the common man, or, if you will, even on fear of him.

Every man is idealistic; only it so often happens that he has the wrong ideal.

It is difficult to attain a high ideal; consequently, it is almost impossible to persuade ourselves that we have attained it.

We are always talking about the sin of intemperate drinking, because it is quite obvious that the poor have it more than the rich. But we are always denying that there is any such thing as the sin of pride, because it would be quite obvious that the rich have it more than the poor.

Heretics (1905)

CLEMENT

Titus Flavius Clemens, also known as Clement of Alexandria, was a Christian convert from paganism who used his knowledge of Greek philosophy to better expound his faith.

His place is preserved in the history of the church by his writings and the work of his students, but information about his life is largely speculative. It is believed he may have been born in Alexandria. A series of chance encounters on his travels may have led to his adopting Christianity. He was ordained sometime before the year 189 AD.

He is generally regarded as a "church father," one of the scholars who helped shape the early church, as are his pupils Origin and Alexander of Jerusalem.

His written works include *The Exhortation* (*Protrepticus*), *The Tutor* (*Paedagogus*), and *The Miscellanies* (*Stromata*).

The Lord, brethren, stands in need of nothing; and He desires nothing of any one, except that confession be made to Him.

Envy and strife have overthrown great cities and rooted up mighty nations.

Let us cleave, therefore, to those who cultivate peace with godliness, and not to those who hypocritically profess to desire it.

Let us then also pray for those who have fallen into any sin, that meekness and humility may be given to them, so that they may submit, not unto us, but to the will of God. For in this way they shall secure a fruitful and perfect remembrance from us, with sympathy for them, both in our prayers to God, and our mention of them to the saints.

Ye see, beloved, how great and wonderful a thing is love, and that there is no declaring its perfection. Who is fit to be found in it, except such as God has vouchsafed to render so? Let us pray, therefore, and implore of His mercy, that we may live blameless in love, free from all human partialities for one above another.

The First Epistle of Clement to the Corinthians (2nd century)

CLOUD, HENRY, AND JOHN TOWNSEND

For the past twenty years, Drs. Henry Cloud and John Townsend have focused their work on helping people find ways to grow personally, professionally, and spiritually. To this end they formed Cloud Townsend Resources.

Dr. Henry Cloud was born in Vicksburg, Massachusetts, in 1956 and is a graduate of Southern Methodist University. He is the leadership director for the American Association of Christian Counselors. Aside from his work with Cloud Townsend, he has a keen interest in homelessness issues and mission development.

Dr. John Townsend, born in Smithfield, North Carolina, in 1952, conducts Leadership Coaching seminars for executives and business owners. He founded a health-care company that operated across thirty-five US cities. He is co-presenter of the nationally syndicated television show *New Life Live*.

Their books include *Boundaries, Now What Do I Do?*, *Who's Pushing Your Buttons?*, and *How People Grow*.

Behaviors have consequences.

Establishing boundaries helps codependent people stop interrupting the Law of Sowing and Reaping in their loved one's life. Boundaries force the person who is doing the sowing to also do the reaping.

Boundaries (1992)

If a person's character makeup determines his future, then child rearing is primarily about helping children to develop character that will take them through life safely, securely, productively, and joyfully.

A major goal of raising children is to help them develop the character that will make their future go well.

Boundaries with Kids (1998)

The perfectionist lives under the Law. He is in bondage to a demand that says, "If you do it right, you'll be loved."

Being confronted on character issues isn't pleasant. It hurts our self-image. It humbles us. But it doesn't harm us. Loving confrontation protects us from blindness and self-destructiveness.

Safe People (2005)

Stay in charge of the only person you can control: yourself.

You can expect to be in control of what you do, but what another person does is totally up to him.

Boundaries Face to Face (2003)

If God is the Creator and we are the creation, we have to depend on Him for life and provision.

Independence is not an option for us. God existed without us, not vice versa.

How People Grow (2001)

We all need to overcome the basic egocentricity of life, the inborn feeling that "the world revolves around me." Whenever we view others only in terms of how they affect us, we are in big trouble.

Don't wait for your spouse to take the first step. Assume the first move is always yours.

Boundaries in Marriage (1999)

No matter what limitation or circumstance you find yourself up against in life, there is a God who can empower you and gift you to go past what you thought was possible. . .when you're at the end of yourself, that's the time He can do His best work.

God does not depend on our willpower and commitment to transform a hopeless situation.

God Will Make a Way (2002)

COLSON, CHARLES

Charles Wendell Colson (known as Chuck) was the first member of the Nixon administration to be jailed on charges relating to the Watergate affair. His conversion to Christianity shortly afterward led to a radical rethinking of his life. He founded Prison Fellowship to spread the Good News to prison inmates and their families.

A new career as a writer and public speaker followed, with all his speaker's fees and royalties being donated to Prison Fellowship.

He founded the Chuck Colson Center for Christian Worldview, and his daily radio broadcast, *BreakPoint*, was heard across the United States.

Born in 1931 in Boston, Massachusetts, he passed away in 2012, spending his last days in Virginia.

His books include *Life Sentence, Born Again, Justice That Restores*, and *The Sky Is Not Falling: Living Fearlessly in These Turbulent Times*.

✍

You are called not to be successful or to meet any of the other counterfeit standards of this world, but to be faithful and to be expended in the cause of serving the risen and returning Christ.

The evidence for the resurrection of Jesus Christ is more powerful than anything else we believe. By His resurrection Jesus proved He is who He says He is. Be confident in this truth. Stand on the Holy Word of God. Don't sell the world a false bill of goods. Preach the Word. Defend the faith. Live the faith.

Faith on the Line (1994)

Abortion is a glaring example of the difference worldview makes. Are not all children—Chinese babies or inner-city African American babies—worthy of protection?

BreakPoint commentary (2009)

Suggest the presence of something outside of and greater than the universe we know, and Darwinists get all but hysterical.

"A Passion for Truth" address (2007)

We reason that we can give in to those seemingly minor temptations—say an emotional attraction to a coworker, or just one drink at the party—because we think we know the boundaries. We think our reason can keep us safe.

Nearly every grave moral failure begins with a small sin.

Are you toying with sin? If so, for yourself, your family, and your Lord—stop. Don't put yourself in a position of compromise.

We humans, you see, have an infinite capacity for self-rationalization.

"The Bewilderment of Sin" address (2009)

We are seeing more and more examples of people treating animals—and even insects—as if they had as much value as humans.

If all life has equal value, then the logical conclusion is to treat all life the same, no matter how lowly—or how deadly, like mosquitoes carrying the West Nile virus.

Christians need to learn to press people to face the logical conclusion of their own beliefs.

"I Got the Sucker" address (2009)

A government cannot be truly just without affirming the intrinsic value of human life.

Kingdoms in Conflict (1987)

Moral crusaders with zeal but no ethical understanding are likely to give us solutions that are worse than the problems.

People who cannot restrain their own baser instincts, who cannot treat one another with civility, are not capable of self-government. . .without virtue, a society can be ruled only by fear, a truth that tyrants understand all too well.

How Now Shall We Live? (2004)

Saving faith—that by which we are justified, made right with God—is a gift of God, and yes, it involves a rational process as well since it comes from hearing the Word of God.

It is impossible to appreciate Jesus apart from the historical context in which He lived.

Loving God (1987)

If the Church has any hope of answering today's challenges, it must pursue what we call radical Christianity or orthodoxy.

We pray that the Kingdom of God will rule in our hearts and once again transform the places in which we live. That will happen only by knowing and living the faith.

The Faith: What Christians Believe, Why They Believe It, and Why It Matters (2008)

To turn away from the great questions and dilemmas of life is a tragedy, for the quest for meaning and truth makes life worth living.

A word of caution: The search for truth and meaning is a lifelong process, and if you ever think you have all the answers, you can become insufferable and dangerous. That is why I still consider myself a seeker. I have passionate convictions, as I've said, but I'm still on a pilgrimage. I'm learning new things every day.

The Good Life (2012)

People who reject transcendent authority can no longer persuade one another through rational arguments; everything is reduced to personal opinion. Debates about ideas thus degenerate into power struggles; we're left with no moral standard by which to measure the common good. For that matter, how can there be a "common good" without an objective standard of truth?

We Christians are to be the best citizens, praying for our leaders and holding them in high regard, even as we push for the reforms desperately needed to keep representative government flourishing.

The Sky Is Not Falling: Living Fearlessly in These Turbulent Times (2011)

DE SALES, FRANCIS

Born in 1567 as the son of a French lord, Francis de Sales initially trained as a magistrate. During his studies he attended a debate on predestination that convinced him he was, in all likelihood, destined for hell. A period of deep depression followed, only lifting when he dedicated himself to the church. In contrast to his initial fears, de Sales's preaching emphasized the loving character of God.

He was an effective evangelist for the Catholic Church during the Protestant Revolution. At the age of thirty-five he was appointed Bishop of Geneva, even though Geneva itself was under Protestant control. He passed away in 1662 in Lyon, France.

His written works (which, unusually for the time, were aimed at the laity) include *Introduction to the Devout Life* and *Treatise on the Love of God*.

Good people who have not as yet attained to devotion fly toward God by their good works but do so infrequently, slowly, and awkwardly. Devout souls ascend to God more frequently, promptly, and with lofty heights. In short, devotion is simply that spiritual agility by which charity works in us or by aid of which we work quickly and lovingly.

Do you seriously wish to travel the road to devotion? If so, look for a good person to guide and lead you.

Charity is spiritual fire, and when it bursts into flames, it is called devotion.

We are crucified to the world, and the world must be as crucified to us. It esteems us as fools, let us esteem it as mad.

To be good a person must have charity, and to be devout, in addition to charity, he must have great zeal and readiness in performing charitable actions.

Introduction to the Devout Life (17th century)

Good will desire for God all the honor, all the glory, and all the recognition that can be rendered Him as a kind of external good due to His goodness.

Just as the rays of the sun do not cease to be true rays when shut out and thrust back by some obstacle, so God's signified will does not cease to be God's true will when we resist it, even though it does not produce as many effects as it would if we had cooperated with it.

Treatise on the Love of God (17th century)

Dobson, James

Born in 1936 in Shreveport, Louisiana, James Dobson is the son, grandson, and great-grandson of ministers. As a child he often traveled with his father on evangelistic tours.

While a student at Pasadena College, he determined to become a Christian psychologist or counselor. He rose to prominence after the publication of *Dare to Discipline* and went on to produce monthly Focus on the Family bulletins. He led the Focus on the Family Foundation until 2003.

Dobson became a powerful player in American politics in the days leading up to the George W. Bush presidency, although his focus was more on promoting church policies than furthering political careers. *Time* magazine called him "the nation's most influential evangelical leader."

His written works include *Dare to Discipline*, *Dr. James Dobson on Parenting*, *Straight Talk to Men*, and *When God Doesn't Make Sense*.

☞

It is time we stand up for what we believe and teach those eternal truths to our children.

The ultimate goal for people of faith is to give each child an understanding of scripture and a lifelong passion for Jesus Christ.

Bringing Up Boys (2001)

There is only one cure for the cancer of bitterness. That is to forgive the perceived offender once and for all, with God's help.

It is not your responsibility to explain what God is doing with your life. He has not provided enough information for you to figure it out. Instead, you are asked to turn loose and let God be God.

When God Doesn't Make Sense (1993)

When you realize that everything you buy is purchased with a portion of your life, it should make you more careful with the use of money.

There is no more important job in the universe than to raise a child to love God, live productively, and serve humanity. How ridiculous that a woman should have to apologize for wanting to fulfill that historic role!

Life on the Edge (1995)

There are qualities in your special youngster that you may not have seen before. Find them. Cultivate them. And then give God time to make something beautiful in their little life.

What a wonderful opportunity it is to teach these little ones to love God with all their heart and to serve fellowman throughout their lives. There is no higher calling than that!

Parenting Isn't for Cowards (1987)

Mothers and fathers are granted a single decade to lay a foundation of values and attitudes by which their children cope with the pressures and problems of adulthood.

The New Hide or Seek (1999)

Children are a gift from God, and we are stewards of their welfare. Training up our daughters in this sense implies helping them to navigate the cultural minefields that lie in their paths—teaching them eternal values, talents, and perspectives. It means instilling within them an appreciation for truthfulness, trustworthiness, self-discipline, self-control, generosity, and sweetness of spirit. It means teaching them modesty, morality, and manners.

Today's little girls are being enticed to grow up too fast and are encountering challenges for which they are totally unprepared.

Bringing Up Girls (2012)

The most vulnerable victims of family instability are the children.

Marital conflict always involves an interaction between two imperfect human beings.

Love Must Be Tough: New Hope for Marriages in Crisis (1996)

Genuine love is not something one "falls" into, as though he or she was tumbling into a ditch. One cannot love an unknown object, regardless of how beautiful or handsome it is. Only when a person begins to develop a deep appreciation for another—an intense awareness of his or her needs, strength, and character—has one begun to experience true love. From there, it should grow for a lifetime.

To experience genuine love with our mate, we must bring a third party into the equation—Jesus Christ. Only through this spiritual connection with Him can we begin to fulfill all the potential of the relationship we call marriage.

Night Light: A Devotional for Couples (2008)

DRUMMOND, HENRY

As a student at Edinburgh University, Scottish-born Henry Drummond was keenly interested in the sciences. His spiritual side was equally exercised by the evangelism of D. L. Moody and Ira D. Sankey.

Drummond would combine these interests to great effect in his book *Natural Law in the Spiritual World*, in which he contended that the laws of nature were continuations of heavenly laws, or evidence of the divine at work. This book appealed to readers both spiritual and secular, providing a middle ground of sorts for the exchange of ideas.

In 1897 he died of bone cancer in Edinburgh, Scotland, at age forty-six. He had a considerable impact on the thinking of his contemporaries and was credited with changing "the spiritual climate of his half-century."

In addition to *Natural Law in the Spiritual World*, Drummond also wrote *The Greatest Thing in the World*, *The Monkey That Would Not Kill*, and *The New Evangelism*.

The peculiarity of ill temper is that it is the vice of the virtuous. It is often the one blot on an otherwise noble character.

There is no suggestion here that religion will absolve any man from bearing burdens. That would be to absolve him from living, since it is life itself that is the burden. What Christianity does propose is to make it tolerable.

Never offer men a thimbleful of Gospel.

All fruits grow—whether they grow in the soil or in the soul; whether they are the fruits of the wild grape or of the True Vine. No man can make things grow. He can get them to grow by arranging all the circumstances and fulfilling all the conditions. But the growing is done by God.

Whenever you attempt a good work you will find other men doing the same kind of work, and probably doing it better. Envy them not.

Banish forever from your minds the idea that religion is subtraction. It does not tell us to give things up, but rather gives us something so much better that they give themselves up.

Humility—to put a seal upon your lips and forget what you have done.

The people who influence you are people who believe in you.

The years of our pilgrimage are all too short to master it triumphantly. Yet this is what Christianity is for—to teach men the art of life.

No worse fate can befall a man in this world than to live and grow old alone, unloving, and unloved.

Love is greater than faith, because the end is greater than the means. What is the use of having faith? It is to connect the soul with God. And what is the object of connecting man with God? That he may become like God. But God is Love. Hence Faith, the means, is in order to Love, the end.

Without distinction, without calculation, without procrastination, love. Lavish it upon the poor, where it is very easy; especially upon the rich, who often need it most; most of all upon our equals, where it is very difficult, and for whom perhaps we each do least of all.

There is no mystery about it. We love others, we love everybody, we love our enemies, because He first loved us.

Why should God have provided that so many hours of every day should be occupied with work? It is because work makes men.

The most obvious lesson in Christ's teaching is that there is no happiness in having and getting anything, but only in giving.

Love not the world therefore. Nothing that it contains is worth the life and consecration of an immortal soul.

If you love, you will unconsciously fulfill the whole law.

The wisdom of the ancients, where is it? It is wholly gone. A schoolboy today knows more than Sir Isaac Newton knew. His knowledge has vanished away.

The Greatest Thing in the World (1874)

Every day as we have prayed, "Thy kingdom come," has our Christian consciousness taken in the tremendous sweep of that prayer and seen how it covers the length and breadth of this great world and every interest of human life?

I started to read the Book to find out what the ideal life was, and I found that the only thing worth doing in the world was to do the will of God; whether that was done in the pulpit or in the slums, whether it was done in the college or classroom or on the street did not matter at all.

It matters little whether we go to foreign lands or stay at home, as long as we are sure that we are where God puts us.

Do not sacrifice yourself to a thing that is disagreeable unless you are quite sure that it is the will of God.

It is your business to restore the integrity and the righteousness in the high places of this land, and let the people see examples which will be helpful to them in their Christian life.

Christians are the only agents God has for carrying out His purposes. Think of that! He could Himself with a single breath cleanse the whole of New York or the whole of London, but He does not do it.

A farm is not a place for growing corn, it is a place for growing character, and a man has no character except what is built up through the medium of the things that he does from day to day.

"My meat and My drink," Christ said, "is to do the will of Him that sent Me," and if you make up your mind that you are going to do the will of God above everything else, it matters little in what direction you work.

The Christian man, simply by virtue of the life that is in him—not by attempting much in the way of forcing it upon others—but by his own spontaneous nature can so work upon men that they cannot but feel that he has been with Jesus.

The only reason that a man should speak at all is because he says things that are not being said.

A Life for a Life and Other Addresses (1893)

Christ is the most gigantic figure of history.

Christ ought to be as near to us as if He were still here. Nothing so simplifies the whole religious life as this thought.

He told us—and it is only because we are so accustomed to it that we do not wonder more at the magnificence of the conception—that when our place in this world should know us no more there would be another place ready for us.

He is training us to a kind of faithfulness whose high quality is unattained by any other earthly means.

Life in the body to all men is short.

There will be no summons of sorrow which He will not be able to answer.

He who seeks God in tangible form misses the very thing he is seeking, for God is a Spirit.

"Why Christ Must Depart" sermon (c. 1890)

One has to do a great deal more than display his Christianity. He must not only talk it, but live it.

Christianity is the great antiseptic of society.

Do not be an amphibian; no man can serve two masters, and, if you only knew it, it is a thousand times easier to seek first the Kingdom of God than to seek it second.

If you want to get a man on his feet again, the thing to do is not to preach or read the Bible to him, but to get him out of the cellar in which he lives. Take him by the hand, and he will be led away from his former life.

Just as in science I should speak of protoplasm, of oxygen or carbonic acid gas, so in talking of religion I must talk about faith and Jesus Christ.

What makes men depressed? Self-concentration, as a rule.

When a man is wrapped up in himself, seeking only his own, he finds he is seeking a very shallow object, and very soon gets to the end of it; hence all the springs of life have nothing to act upon, and depression follows.

Sin is abashed in the presence of Christ.

Be in the company of good books, beautiful pictures, and charming, delightful, and inspiring music; and let all that one hears, sees, reads, and thinks lift and inspire the higher.

Temptation is a pitiless thing. It goes into the church and picks off the man in the pulpit. It goes into the university and picks off the flower of the class.

Many a man goes through life hanging his head with shame and living without his self-respect because he has never discovered the distinction between temptation and sin.

In talking to a man you want to win, talk to him in his own language.

Let a man remember that the great thing is not to think about religion, but to do it.

Stones Rolled Away and Other Addresses to Young Men (1893)

Many long for life to be done that they may rest, as they say, in the quiet grave. Let no cheap sentimentalism deceive us. Death can only be gain when to have lived was Christ.

In the perspective of Eternity all lives will seem poor, and small, and lost, and self-condemned beside a life for Christ.

The time will come when we shall ask ourselves why we ever crushed this infinite substance of our life within these narrow bounds, and centered that which lasts forever on what must pass away.

"To Me to Live Is Christ" sermon (c. 1890)

Life cannot come gradually—health can, structure can, but not Life.

Life is definite and resident; and Spiritual Life is not a visit from a force, but a resident tenant in the soul.

Each man has only a certain amount of life, of time, of attention—a definite measurable quantity. If he gives any of it to this life solely it is wasted.

The discipline of life was meant to destroy this self, but that discipline having been evaded—and we all to some extent have opportunities, and too often exercise them, of taking the narrow path by the shortest cuts—its purpose is baulked. But the soul is the loser.

If we neglect the opportunities for cultivating the mind, how shall it escape ignorance and feebleness?

The greatest truths are always the most loosely held.

The religion of Jesus has probably always suffered more from those who have misunderstood than from those who have opposed it.

No man is called to a life of self-denial for its own sake.

The penalty of evading self-denial is just that we get the lesser instead of the larger good.

So long as the regenerate man is kept in this world, he must find the old environment at many points a severe temptation.

Natural Law in the Spiritual World (c. 1884)

So Godlike a gift is intellect, so wondrous a thing is consciousness, that to link them with the animal world seems to trifle with the profoundest distinctions in the Universe.

Lowell Lectures on the Ascent of Man (1893)

"To me to live is—business"; "to me to live is—pleasure," "to me to live is—myself." We can all tell in a moment what our religion is really worth. "To me to live is"—what? What are we living for? What rises naturally in our heart when we press it with a test like this: "to me to live is"—what?

Ideal Life (1890)

EDWARDS, JONATHAN

Born in 1703 in East Windsor, Connecticut, Jonathan Edwards was the fifth of eleven children. He was educated by his older siblings and his parents before attending Yale College at the age of thirteen. He later became a tutor there.

At the age of twenty-six, upon the death of his grandfather, who had been the minister there, Edwards took sole ministerial charge of Northampton in Massachusetts. In later years he found himself at odds with his congregation and was eventually removed from his post. Despite offers of other positions, he chose instead to become a missionary to the Housatonic Indians, whose rights he championed. He died in 1758 trying to prevent a smallpox epidemic in Princeton, New Jersey.

He is generally considered one of America's greatest theologians and, possibly, its greatest intellectual.

His many written works include *A Treatise Concerning Religious Affections*, *Charity and Its Fruits*, *The Nature of True Virtue*, and *Original Sin*.

If we are not disposed meekly to bear injuries, we are not fitted to live in the world, for in it we must expect to meet with many injuries from men.

Love to God disposes men to see His hand in everything; to own Him as the governor of the world, and the director of providence; and to acknowledge His disposal in everything that takes place.

When it is said that charity suffers long, we cannot infer from this, that we are to bear injuries meekly for a season, and that after that season we may cease thus to bear them.

It is pride or self-conceit, that is very much the foundation of a high and bitter resentment, and of an unforgiving and revengeful spirit.

"Charity Disposes Us Meekly to Bear the Injuries Received
from Others" sermon (1738)

What an indecent self-exaltation and arrogance it is, in poor, fallible, dark mortals, to pretend that they can determine and know, who are really sincere and upright before God, and who are not!

It is not God's design that men should obtain assurance in any other way, than by mortifying corruption, and increasing in grace, and obtaining the lively exercises of it.

The strong and lively exercises of a spirit of childlike, evangelical, humble love to God, give clear evidence of the soul's relation to God as his child; which does very greatly and directly satisfy the soul.

The true saints have not such a spirit of discerning that they can certainly determine who are godly, and who are not. For though they know experimentally what true religion is, in the internal exercises of it; yet these are what they can neither feel, nor see, in the heart of another.

It is men's duty to love all whom they are bound in charity to look upon as the children of God, with a vastly dearer affection than they commonly do.

As gold that is tried in the fire, is purged from its alloy, and all remainders of dross, and comes forth more solid and beautiful; so true faith being tried as gold is tried in the fire, becomes more precious, and thus also is "found unto praise, and honor, and glory."

False religion may cause persons to be loud and earnest in prayer.

The Spirit of God is given to the true saints to dwell in them, as his proper lasting abode; and to influence their hearts, as a principle of new nature or as a divine supernatural spring of life and action.

Surely God is so sovereign as that comes to, that He may enable us to do our duty when He pleases, and on what occasion He pleases.

God's manner is not to bring comfortable texts of scripture to give men assurance of His love, and that they shall be happy, before they have had a faith of dependence.
No promise of the covenant of grace belongs to any man, until he has first believed in Christ.

When God sets His seal on a man's heart by His Spirit, there is some holy stamp, some image impressed and left upon the heart by the Spirit, as by the seal upon the wax.

Grace is the godly man's treasure.

Grace in the hearts of the saints, being therefore the most glorious work of God, wherein He communicates of the goodness of His nature, it is doubtless His peculiar work, and in an eminent manner above the power of all creatures.

It is God's manner of dealing with men, to "lead them into a wilderness, before He speaks comfortably to them," and so to order it, that they shall be brought into distress, and made to see their own helplessness and absolute dependence on His power and grace, before He appears to work any great deliverance for them, is abundantly manifest by the scripture.

Men in a corrupt and carnal frame have their spiritual senses in but poor plight for judging and distinguishing spiritual things.

When true Christians are in an ill frame, guilt lies on the conscience; which will bring fear, and so prevent the peace and joy of an assured hope.

A true saint greatly delights in holiness; it is a most beautiful thing in his eyes; and God's work, in savingly renewing and making holy and happy, a poor, and before perishing soul, appears to him a most glorious work.

There are no other principles, which human nature is under the influence of, that will ever make men conscientious, but one of these two, fear or love.

The hypocrite has not the knowledge of his own blindness, and the deceitfulness of his own heart, and that mean opinion of his own understanding that the true saint has.

The devil does not assault the hope of the hypocrite, as he does the hope of a true saint.

A man must first love God or have his heart united to him, before he will esteem God's good his own, and before he will desire the glorifying, and enjoying of God as his happiness.
Men may love a God of their own forming in their imaginations, when they are far from loving such a God as reigns in heaven.

When once a hypocrite is thus established in a false hope, he has not those things to cause him to call his hope in question, that oftentimes are the occasion of the doubting of true saints.

True virtue never appears so lovely, as when it is most oppressed; and the divine excellency of real Christianity, is never exhibited with such advantage, as when under the greatest trials.

How great therefore may the resemblance be, as to all outward expressions and appearances, between a hypocrite and a true saint!

The only certain foundation which any person has to believe that he is invited to partake of the blessings of the gospel, is, that the word of God declares that persons so qualified as he is, are invited, and God who declares it, is true, and cannot lie.

Christians in their effectual calling, are not called to idleness, but to labor in God's vineyard, and spend their day in doing a great and laborious service.

Doubtless it is the glorious prerogative of the omniscient God, as the great searcher of hearts, to be able well to separate between sheep and goats.

Conscience naturally gives men an apprehension of right and wrong, and suggests the relation there is between right and wrong, and a retribution: the Spirit of God assists men's consciences to do this in a greater degree, helps conscience against the stupefying influence of worldly objects and their lusts.

A Treatise Concerning Religious Affections (c. 1750)

There is an absolute and universal dependence of the redeemed on God.

The great power of God appears in bringing a sinner from his low state, from the depths of sin and misery, to such an exalted state of holiness and happiness.

It is a more glorious work of power to rescue a soul out of the hands of the devil, and from the powers of darkness, and to bring it into a state of salvation, than to confer holiness where there was no prepossession or opposition.
By its being thus ordered, that the creature should have so absolute and universal a dependence on God, provision is made that God should have our whole souls, and should be the object of our undivided respect.

It is necessary in order to saving faith, that man should be emptied of himself, be sensible that he is "wretched, and miserable, and poor, and blind, and naked." Humility is a great ingredient of true faith.

Faith abases men, and exalts God; it gives all the glory of redemption to Him alone.

Success depends entirely and absolutely on the immediate blessing and influence of God.

The grace of God in bestowing this gift is most free. It was what God was under no obligation to bestow.

Christ is the true light of the world; it is through him alone that true wisdom is imparted to the mind.

It is by God's power that we are preserved in a state of grace.

"God Glorified in Man's Dependence" sermon (1731)

If we make a great show of respect and love to God, in the outward actions, while there is no sincerity in the heart, it is but hypocrisy and practical lying unto the Holy One.

To pretend to such respect and love, when it is not felt in the heart, is to act as if we thought we could deceive God.

When a man has given away all his goods, he has nothing else remaining that he can give, but himself.

Whatever is done or suffered, yet if the heart is withheld from God, there is nothing really given to Him.

Whatever men may do or suffer, they cannot by all their performances and sufferings, make up for the want of sincere love in the heart.

A cup of cold water given to a disciple in sincere love, is worth more in God's sight, than all one's goods given to feed the poor, yea, than the wealth of a kingdom given away, or a body offered up in the flames without love.

> "The Greatest Performances or Sufferings in Vain without Charity" sermon (1738)

The heartfelt praises of one true believer are more precious to God than all the 220,000 oxen and the 120,000 sheep that Solomon offered to God at the dedication of the temple.

Earthly things need to be ignored and despised by those of heavenly descent.

> "Christians, a Royal Priesthood" sermon (1744)

What is it that chiefly makes you desire to go to heaven when you die?

> "God, the Best Portion of Christians" sermon (1744)

The final judgment will be done to display and glorify the righteousness of God.

Everything in the gospel is ordered by God to extend the maximum grace and mercy to His people.

> "The Final Judgment" sermon (1741)

If believers are truly chosen by God, they should be grateful.

> "Christians—A Chosen Generation" sermon (1742)

Eternity depends on the proper use of time.

"The Preciousness of Time and the Importance
of Redeeming It" sermon (1734)

How does the wise man die? As does the fool.

Every man plots how he may escape damnation.

Sin is the ruin and misery of the soul. It is destructive in its nature, and if God should leave it without restraint, nothing else would be needed to make the soul miserable.

The unconverted walk over the pit of hell on a rotten bridge.

Natural men are held in the hand of God over the pit of hell.

There is nothing that keeps wicked men, at any one moment, out of hell, but the mere pleasure of God.

The bow of God's wrath is bent, and the arrow is made ready on the string, and justice bends the arrow at your heart.

O sinner! Consider the fearful danger you are in: 'tis a great furnace of wrath, a wide and bottomless pit.

"Sinners in the Hands of an Angry God" sermon (1741)

Christ is at all times totally sufficient for the office He has undertaken.

"Jesus Christ, the Same Yesterday, Today, and Forever"
sermon (1744)

ELLIOT, ELISABETH

Born in Belgium to missionaries in 1926, Elisabeth Howard was studying classical Greek in college with a view to translating the New Testament when she met her husband-to-be, Jim Elliot. Later they were married in Ecuador, where they were both working with the Quichua tribe.

Her husband was killed in 1952 (along with four other men) by the Auca Indians they were seeking to evangelize. To the amazement of the world, Mrs. Elliot later returned to the area and spent two years working with the Aucas.

A prolific writer, she was a style consultant on the committee that compiled the NIV Bible.

Her many books include *Shadow of the Almighty*, *The Life and Testament of Jim Elliot*, *The Savage My Kinsman*, *The Mark of a Man*, and *Taking Flight: Wisdom for Your Journey*.

The deepest lessons come out of the deepest waters and the hottest fires.

Each time the mystery of suffering touches us personally and all the cosmic questions arise fresh in our minds we face the choice between faith (which accepts) and unbelief (which refuses to accept).

A Path through Suffering (1990)

Most of the time we like the idea of our own freedom. There are times when we do not at all like the idea of the freedom of others. If we suffer because of their freedom, let us remember that they suffer because of ours.

The power to exercise the will has been delegated to us and God will not usurp it.

These Strange Ashes (1989)

I will offer to Him both my tears and my exultation. Nothing we offer to Him will be lost.

It takes the deep water and the hot fire and the dark valley to teach us the walk of faith.

Be Still My Soul (2003)

In order to learn what it means to be a woman, we must start with the One who made her.

If you believe in a God who controls the big things, you have to believe in a God who controls the little things. It is we, of course, to whom things look "little" or "big."

Let Me Be a Woman (1976)

For the Christian there is one rule and one rule only: total abstention from sexual activity outside of marriage and total faithfulness inside marriage. Period.

Waiting silently is the hardest thing of all.

Passion and Purity (1984)

Refresh me today in Your love, so that in Your coolness I may stand the heat.

Fear arises when we imagine that everything depends on us.

The Music of His Promises (2000)

Our Heavenly Healer often has to hurt us in order to heal us. We sometimes fail to recognize His mighty love in this, yet we are firmly held always in the Everlasting Arms.

Have we the humility to thank our Father for the gift of pain?

Secure in the Everlasting Arms (2002)

Eve was declaring her rights. What she saw as her rights had nothing to do with the will of God and therefore nothing to do, finally, with her happiness, sure as she was that they had.

When the Constitution declares that "all men are created equal," it is not referring to intelligence, good looks, good humor, height, weight, or income. It is talking about certain rights, "inalienable" in that they cannot be taken away.

The Mark of a Man (1981)

The father is the priest in the home. This means standing in the presence of God for others. It means making sacrifices on their behalf. In a deep spiritual sense he stands in the place of God in the home—His representative, the visible sign of His presence, His love, His care.

The establishment of a child's trust in God begins with his trust in the word of his parents.

The Shaping of the Christian Family (1992)

EVANS, TONY

In 1976 Anthony T. Evans founded Oak Cliff Bible Fellowship. What began as a home church with only ten people grew into a megachurch with more than ninety-seven hundred members and a hundred ministries.

Dr. Evans aims to change the world by enabling people to empower their churches to change their communities. To this end he helped found (and became president of) the Urban Alternative program.

In addition to being pastor for the Dallas Cowboys, Dr. Evans is an in-demand speaker and broadcaster. His radio show, *The Alternative with Dr. Tony Evans*, is broadcast in over eighty countries. He is a regular speaker at Promise Keepers conventions.

His books include *The Truth about Angels and Demons*, *Returning to Your First Love*, *Totally Saved*, and *Guiding Your Family in a Misguided World*.

✍

From the first word of Genesis to the last word of Revelation, God's Word is true and trustworthy. All we need do is obey the words of Jesus and abide in that Word and we'll have an answer for any lie or temptation Satan throws our way.

Satan is a liar, a deceiver, and a counterfeiter. And it's important for all of us to know that he's real and that he's doing everything he can to make our walk with Jesus and our witness for Him ineffective.

God Cannot Be Trusted (And Five Other Lies of Satan) (2005)

It's important to God, and therefore to us, that we be intentional about how we train our children, especially in light of the way our culture would mislead them.

There are no shortcuts when it comes to building a healthy, loving, and caring family.

Guiding Your Family (1991)

Satan has a definite strategy, and it can be understood in one word: deception.

Commitment doesn't work unless it's preceded by surrender. Commitment often says, "I can," but surrender says, "Lord, I can't."

Tony Evans Speaks Out (2000)

To give you an idea of the depth of Jesus' suffering, being abandoned by God is the definition of hell.

Because Jesus Christ is a man, He feels what we feel. Because He is God, He can do something about it.

Theology You Can Count On (2008)

Seek the welfare of others. Find out how you can be a blessing. Pray for the city you live in right now and its people, for its welfare and your welfare. This is one of the fundamental keys. As you become a blessing, you set yourself up to be blessed.

What's amazing is that the grace of God is so far-reaching and profound that He can use your failures.

God Is Up to Something Great (2002)

Because of the Holy Spirit's witness and illumination, you neve
alone in your decisions—but this is true only as long as you're
mind of God and wanting to do His will.

How do you know when you're walking in the Spirit? You know it when
you're living a life of prayer, because prayer is the proof of dependence on
the Spirit.

The Fire That Ignites (2003)

FÉNELON, FRANÇOIS AND JEANNE GUYON

Born in 1651 in Sainte-Mondane, France, François Fénelon was a poet, theologian, and Archbishop of Cambrai. He was also known as a reformer and defender of human rights. During the Protestant Reformation his skills as an orator led to his being sent to troubled parts of France to restore peace and bring "wayward" Protestants back to the Catholic flock.

He became a devotee and protector of Madame Guyon, who was an advocate of Quietism, a philosophy of faith that emphasized spiritual stillness, contemplation, and passivity. The church declared it a heretical practice, and Madame Guyon was jailed for eight years after publishing a book in support of the practice.

Fénelon died in 1715 in Cambrai, France. His written works include *The Adventures of Telemachus*.

Madame Guyon, who was born in 1648 in Montargis, France, died in 1717, in Blois, France. Her written works include *A Short and Easy Method of Prayer*.

☞

Those who have stations of importance to fill, have generally so many indispensable duties to perform, that without the greatest care in the management of their time, none will be left to be alone with God.

What a contrast! Nothingness strives to be something, and the Omnipotent becomes nothing! I will be nothing with Thee, my Lord!

It is true that He desires our happiness, but that is neither the chief end of His work, nor an end to be compared with that of His glory.

cost what it may, and in spite of my fears and speculations, I desire to become lowly and a fool, still more despicable in my own eyes than in those of the wise in their own conceit.

True humility consists in a deep view of our utter unworthiness, and in an absolute abandonment to God, without the slightest doubt that He will do the greatest things in us.

Thou art the life of my soul as my soul is the life of my body.

Thou art more intimately present to me than I am to myself; this I, to which I am so attached and which I have so ardently loved, ought to be strange to me in comparison with Thee; Thou art the bestower of it.

Give every truth time to send down deep roots into the heart.

One of the cardinal rules of the spiritual life is that we are to live exclusively in the present moment, without casting a look beyond.

The wise and diligent traveler watches all his steps, and keeps his eyes always directed to that part of the road which is immediately before him; but he does not incessantly look backwards to count his steps and examine his footmarks.

Again I warn you, beware of philosophers and great reasoners. They will always be a snare to you, and will do you more harm than you will know how to do them good. They linger and pine away in discussing exterior trifles, and never reach the knowledge of the truth.

Let us enjoy light and consolation when it is His pleasure to give it to us, but let us not attach ourselves to His gifts, but to Him; and when He plunges us into the night of Pure Faith, let us still press on through the agonizing darkness.

Never trouble yourself to inquire whether you will have strength to endure what is presented, if it should actually come upon you, for the moment of trial will have its appointed and sufficient grace.

We should choose those works for reading which instruct us in our duty and in our faults; which, while they point out the greatness of God, teach us what is our duty to Him, and how very far we are from performing it; not those barren productions which melt and sentimentalize the heart.

It is not necessary to descend into the depths nor to pass beyond the seas; it is not necessary to ascend into the heavens to find Thee; Thou art nearer to us than we are to ourselves.

What men stand most in need of is the knowledge of God.

Never should we so abandon ourselves to God as when He seems to abandon us.

Let me, O my God, stifle forever in my heart, every thought that would tempt me to doubt Thy goodness.

Let us pray God that He would root out of our hearts everything of our own planting, and set out there, with His own hands, the tree of life, bearing all manner of fruits.

We should be faithless indeed, and guilty of heathen distrust, did we desire to penetrate the future, which God has hidden from us; leave it to Him: let Him make it short or long, bitter or sweet; let Him do with it even as it shall please Himself.

We must prefer God before ourselves, and endeavor to will our own happiness for His glory.

Spiritual Progress (17th century)

Peace of conscience, liberty of heart, the sweetness of abandoning ourselves in the hands of God, the joy of always seeing the light grow in our hearts, finally, freedom from the fears and insatiable desires of the times, multiply a hundredfold the happiness which the true children of God possess in the midst of their crosses, if they are faithful.

What God asks of us is a will which is no longer divided between Him and any creature. It is a will pliant in His hands which neither seeks nor rejects anything, which wants without reserve whatever He wants, and which never wants under any pretext anything which He does not want.

How dangerous it is for our salvation, how unworthy of God and of ourselves, how pernicious even for the peace of our hearts, to want always to stay where we are! Our whole life was only given us to advance us by great strides toward our heavenly country.

The love of God, which will make us conscious of God's love for us, will give us wings to fly on His way and to raise us above all our troubles.

There is only one way to love God: to take not a single step without Him, and to follow with a brave heart wherever He leads.

Christian Perfection (17th century)

FINNEY, CHARLES

Charles Grandison Finney, born in 1792 in Warren, Connecticut, was known as the father of modern revivalism, although "modern" times for him were the eighteenth and nineteenth centuries. He was a social reformer and advocate of equal rights for women and African-Americans.

He practiced law but came to the faith and was ordained as a Presbyterian minister at the age of twenty-nine. He became known for his innovative style of preaching, including mixed-sex gatherings, women leading prayers, and the public naming of individuals in his sermons.

In 1851 he was named president of Oberlin College in Ohio and encouraged the education of different races and both sexes in the same classes. He died in 1875 in Oberlin.

His written works include *Lectures on Revivals of Religion*, *Views of Sanctification*, and *Lectures on Systematic Theology*.

☝

Be honest about it. Would you take all these pains about your looks if everybody was blind?

Confess to God those sins that have been committed against God, and to man those sins that have been committed against man.

Because sinners are not converted by direct contact of the Holy Ghost, but by the truth, employed as a means. To expect the conversion of sinners by prayer alone, without the employment of truth, is to tempt God.

Understand now what lying is. Any species of designed deception. If the deception is not designed it is not lying. But if you design to make an impression contrary to the naked truth, you lie.

It will do no good to preach to you while your hearts are in this hardened, and wasted, and fallow state. The farmer might just as well sow his grain on the rock. It will bring forth no fruit.

There are many professors who are willing to do almost anything in religion, that does not require self-denial.

Unbelief. Instances in which you have virtually charged the God of truth with lying, by your unbelief of his express promises and declarations.

Lectures of Revivals of Religion (1835)

It seems to be a law of man's intelligent nature that when accused of wrong, either by his conscience or by any other agent, he must either confess or justify.

Real hardness of heart, in the Bible use of the phrase, means stubbornness of will.

Let me ask you, sinner, how much time will it take you to do the first great duty which God requires, namely, give Him your heart?

No sinner under the light of the Gospel lives a single hour in sin without some excuse, either tacit or avowed, by which he justifies himself.

You can't make up your mind now to break off from all sin. If this be really so, then you cannot make up your mind to obey God, and you may as well make up your mind to go to hell! There is no alternative!

"The Sinner's Excuses Answered" sermon (c. 1850)

You hear the word, and believe it in theory, while you deny it in practice. I say to you, that "you deceive yourselves."

There is that fear of the Lord which is the beginning of wisdom, which is founded in love. There is also a slavish fear, which is a mere dread of evil, and is purely selfish.

The reason why wicked men and devils hate God is, because they see Him in relation to themselves. Their hearts rise up in rebellion, because they see Him opposed to their selfishness.

The end for which Christ lives, and for which He has left His church in the world, is the salvation of sinners.

If you are not growing in grace, becoming more and more holy, yielding yourselves up to the influence of the gospel, you are deceiving yourselves.

There are two classes of hypocrites among professors of religion, those that deceive others and those that deceive themselves.

Those who are always ready to ask how little they may do for religion rather than how much they may do, are serving their own gods.

When a man's understanding is convinced, and he admit the truth in its relation to himself, then there must be a hearty approbation of it in its bearing or relation to himself.

To serve God is to make religion the main business of life.

Lectures to Professing Christians (1837)

I looked to God with great earnestness day after day, to be directed; asking Him to show me the path of duty, and give me grace to ride out the storm.

Unless I had the spirit of prayer I could do nothing. If even for a day or an hour I lost the spirit of grace and supplication, I found myself unable to preach with power and efficiency, or to win souls by personal conversation.

Memoirs of Rev. Charles G. Finney (1876)

Nothing can be a more grievous abomination in the sight of God than excuses made by a sinner who knows they are utterly false and blasphemous.

Often, without being at all aware of it, men judge themselves, not by God's rule, but by their own.

The world's entire morality and that of a large portion of the Church are only a spurious benevolence.

The highest forms of the world's morality are only abominations in God's sight.

"Men Often Highly Esteem What God Abhors" sermon (c. 1850)

The truth is, God is the most reasonable of all beings. He asks only that we should use each moment for Him, in labor, or in rest, whichever is most for His glory. He only requires that with the time, talents, and strength which He has given us, we should do all we can to serve Him.

Sermons on Gospel Themes (1850)

FLAVEL, JOHN

John Flavel was born in 1627 in Bromsgrove, England. In his early twenties he was appointed assistant to a minister in Devon, England. He endeared himself to the parishioners through his friendliness and more tolerant approach to their financial situations when it came to tithes.

Due to the changing political climate, he was twice removed from his position as minister. Both times he continued to preach nearby, and many of his ex-parishioners joined his new congregations. At one point he organized a church from his home in Dartmouth until his flock built him a meetinghouse in defiance of the church authorities. He passed away in 1691 in Exeter, England.

His written works include *Husbandry Spiritualized, A Saint Indeed, The Seaman's Companion, Pneumatologia: A Treatise on the Soul of Man,* and *Gospel Unity: Recommended to the Churches of Christ.*

God has endued the soul of man not only with an understanding to discern, and direct, but also a will to govern, moderate, and overrule the actions of life.

The soul of man, like the bird in the shell, is still growing or ripening in sin or grace, till at last the shell breaks by death, and the soul flies away to the piece it is prepared for, and where it must abide forever.

"They cannot kill the soul." And though the Almighty power of God, that created it out of nothing, can as easily reduce it to nothing; yet He will never do so.

My soul is of more value than ten thousand worlds.

The will, like an absolute sovereign, reigns over the body.

The soul of the poorest child is of equal dignity with the soul of Adam.

He only that stills the stormy seas, can quiet the distressed and tempestuous soul.

The voice of conscience is the voice of God; for it is his vicegerent and representative.

We are not distinguished from brutes by our senses, but by our understanding.

Pneumatologia (1698)

As all the rivers are gathered into the ocean, which is the meeting-place of all the waters in the world, so Christ is that ocean in which all true delights and pleasures meet.

Creatures, like pictures, are fairest at a certain distance, but it is not so with Christ; the nearer the soul approaches Him, and the longer it lives in the enjoyment of Him, still the sweeter and more desirable He becomes.

He feels all our sorrows, needs, and burdens as his own. This is why it is said that the sufferings of believers are called the sufferings of Christ.

If a small measure of grace in the saints makes them sweet and desirable companions, what must the riches of the Spirit of grace filling Jesus Christ without measure make Him in the eyes of believers?

The best creature-comfort apart from Christ is but a broken cistern. It cannot hold one drop of true comfort.

He is bread to the hungry, water to the thirsty, a garment to the naked, healing to the wounded; and whatever a soul can desire is found in Him.

Christ comes with kingly power, to rescue sinners, as a prey from the mouth of the terrible one.

We have no beauty, no goodness to make us desirable in His eyes; all the origins of His love to us are in His own breast.

If a pardon be sweet to a condemned criminal, how sweet must the sprinkling of the blood of Jesus be to the trembling conscience of a law-condemned sinner?

We are, by nature, blind and ignorant, at best but groping in the dim light of nature after God.

Christ Altogether Lovely (c. 1670)

FOSTER, RICHARD

Born in 1942 in New Mexico, Richard Foster is a professor at Friends University in Wichita (an educational establishment with links to the Society of Friends). He writes in a Quaker style but his books have an across-the-board appeal.

He founded Renovaire, a nonprofit organization designed to help churches and individuals become more Christlike. The organization works in many countries and with many denominations.

His book *Celebration of Discipline*, which outlines many of the principles upon which Renovaire operates, was named as one of the top ten books of the twentieth century by *Christianity Today*.

In addition to *Celebration of Discipline*, his books include *Streams of Living Water*, *Sanctuary of the Soul*, and *Freedom of Simplicity*.

✍

Because we lack a divine Center our need for security has led us into an insane attachment to things.

In intellectual honesty, we should be willing to study and explore the spiritual life with all the rigor and determination we would give to any field of research.

Celebration of Discipline (1978)

If you seek holiness of life, I encourage you to make a good friend of the sermon on the mount.

It is a genuine act of humility to realize that we can learn from others who have gone before us.

Streams of Living Water (1998)

Jesus Christ and all the writers of the New Testament call us to break free of mammon lust and live in joyous trust.... They point us toward a way of living in which everything we have we receive as a gift, and everything we have is cared for by God, and everything we have is available to others when it is right and good. This reality frames the heart of Christian simplicity. It is the means of liberation and power to do what is right and to overcome the forces of fear and avarice.

And so I urge you to still every motion that is not rooted in the Kingdom.

Freedom of Simplicity: Finding Harmony in a Complex World (2005)

Today the heart of God is an open wound of love. He aches over our distance and preoccupation. He mourns that we do not draw near to Him. He grieves that we have forgotten Him. He weeps over our obsession with muchness and manyness. He longs for our presence.

He is inviting you—and me—to come home, to come home to where we belong, to come home to that for which we were created. His arms are stretched out wide to receive us. His heart is enlarged to take us in.

Prayer: Finding the Heart's True Home (2002)

The crying need today is for people of faith to live faithfully. This is true in all spheres of human existence, but is particularly true with reference to money, sex, and power. No issues touch us more profoundly or more universally.

Jesus did not give detailed instruction on how we are to live in every corner of life. Instead He took the crucial issues of His day and showed how the gospel message bears upon them.

The Challenge of the Disciplined Life: Christian Reflections on Money, Sex, and Power (1989)

GEORGE, ELIZABETH

Elizabeth George, born in 1944, is a Christian writer whose many books encourage women to live lives of faith and study the Bible. Her strength lies in helping women apply biblical principles in their everyday lives.

She and her husband, Jim, run a joint ministry: Elizabeth caring for women, Jim encouraging men. More than eight million copies of their books have been sold. She is a regular speaker at conferences and women's retreats. She also broadcasts a regular radio program called *A Minute for Busy Women*.

Her books include *A Woman after God's Own Heart*, *A Young Woman Who Reflects the Heart of Jesus*, and *One-Minute Inspirations for Women*.

Find the gold. Whatever has happened to you in the past, and whatever is happening in your life now, look for the hidden blessing, the lesson to be learned, or the character trait to be forged. Trust that, since God has allowed these experiences, somewhere there is gold for you.

Because He is God, He is able to weave together every single aspect and event in your life and produce something good.

Loving God with All Your Mind (1994)

You and I can go to God when we are too tired, too lazy, too uncommitted, too sick, or feeling too sorry for ourselves. In fact, moments like these are precisely when we need to call upon God and be filled with His faithfulness.

Our days are in God's hands. He is all-sufficient to meet our needs, and the Savior is with us every step of the way.

God's Garden of Grace (1996)

Choose God's ways at every opportunity.

Decide to make your husband your number-one human relationship.

A Woman after God's Own Heart (1997)

So why do we worry? Why do we worry about food and clothing? About finances and money? About security and the needs of life? We have Jehovah-Rohi! We have the Lord as our caring Shepherd. When fears regarding the cares of this world set in, we need to confidently lean on God's promise to care for us. Then we can declare to God, "Whenever I am afraid, I will trust in You" (Psalm 56:3).

With the help of the Lord, you can handle life's challenges and heartaches, even the valley of the shadow of death. What comfort your fainting heart has, knowing that in those stumbling times of discouragement and despair, of depletion and seeming defeat, the Shepherd will find you. . .restore and "fix" you. . .and follow you. . .until you are well on your way.

Quiet Confidence for a Woman's Heart (2009)

For every need and issue and decision that must be made in life, the Bible has the answers.

God's Word is exciting, so electric, so energizing.

God's Wisdom for a Woman's Life: Timeless Principles
for Your Every Need (2003)

Like completing a run, living today begins with preparation, planning, and prayer.

Loving God with All Your Mind (2005)

Worry denies the power of God and produces no good results. Worry adds no value to your life. Eliminate it with God's help.

Replace worry with prayer. Make the decision to pray whenever you catch yourself worrying.

Breaking the Worry Habit. . .Forever! God's Plan
for Lasting Peace of Mind (2009)

Just as mental toughness and physical energy are the primary traits of an army, they also mark God's beautiful woman.

God values Christian character, which shines in positive, outward conduct. Fashion your heart after Jesus.

Walking with the Women of the Bible:
A Devotional Journey through God's Word (2008)

A godly woman is beyond average because she keeps her word. She honors her vows. She exhibits great faith. She overcomes great obstacles. And she affects her family, her community, even the world.

Dust off that Bible. It has the answers you are looking for, and its delights await you.

A Woman's Daily Walk with God (2012)

The soul of a child is the loveliest flower that grows in the garden of God.

A Mom after God's Own Heart: 10 Ways to Love Your Children (2012)

God has given you the stewardship of raising your daughter to follow Him, to train her up in the way she should go. And He's given you everything you need for the job: His principles and instructions right out of His Word.

Raising a Daughter after God's Own Heart (2011)

GORDON, SAMUEL D.

Born in 1859 in Philadelphia, Pennsylvania, Samuel Dickey Gordon was that rare creature: a man who lived and talked about God's will in a way that earned the respect of all, without ever being ordained or trained in theology. A simple man, he was described as perfectly balanced in the Word and in the Spirit.

Samuel wrote more than twenty-five books, most of them in the "Quiet Talks" series, a name that reflected his own manner of speech. He worked for the YMCA and spent several years traveling Asia visiting mission fields. His books were extremely popular before World War I. He would produce two a year and spend the rest of his time giving lectures on them. He lived until 1936.

His books include *Quiet Talks on Service*, *Quiet Talks on Prayer*, and *Quiet Talks about Jesus*.

With due reverence, but very plainly, let it be said that God can do nothing for the man with shut hand and shut life. There must be an open hand and heart and life through which God can give what He longs to.

If there be but one in a home in touch with God, that one becomes God's door into the whole family.

God is eagerly watching with hungry eyes for the quick turn of a human eye up to Himself.

Philosophically there must be a hell. That is the name for the place where God is not; for the place where they will gather together who insist on leaving God out. God out! There can be no worse hell than that! God away! Man held back by no restraints!

Prayer is striking the winning blow at the concealed enemy. Service is gathering up the results of that blow among the men we see and touch.

An open life, an open hand, open upward, is the pipe line of communication between the heart of God and this poor befooled old world.

The purpose of prayer is to get God's will done.

The heart of God hungers to redeem the world.

We cannot know a man's mental processes. This is surely true, that if in the very last half-twinkling of an eye a man look up towards God longingly, that look is the turning of the will to God. And that is quite enough.

The real victory in all of this service is won in secret, beforehand, by prayer.

Quiet Talks on Prayer (1904)

GRAHAM, BILLY

In 1918 William Franklin Graham was born into an Associate Reformed Presbyterian Church family in Charlotte, North Carolina, and raised on a dairy farm. Considered too worldly for a youth group in his teens, he also found the teaching at Bob Jones College too legalistic. But the founder of the college, Bob Jones Sr., encouraged him to curb his rebellious streak, insisting that greater things lay in store for him.

He took the founder's words to heart and eventually was ordained as a pastor while still at college. Later he went on to become an evangelist, traveling the States and abroad. Eventually his "crusades" brought him worldwide attention. It is estimated that he has preached to more than 2.2 billion people. He has also served as a spiritual advisor to many US presidents.

His books include *Calling Youth to Christ, Storm Warning, Just as I Am,* and *Nearing Home: Life, Faith, and Finishing Well.*

✍

Angels minister to us personally. Many accounts in scripture confirm that we are the subjects of their individual concern.

We may not always be aware of the presence of angels. We can't always predict how they will appear. But angels have been said to be our neighbors. Often they may be our companions without our being aware of their presence. We know little of their constant ministry.

Angels (1975)

God doesn't comfort us to make us comfortable, but to make us comforters.

A lot of people talk about hell, use it to tell others where to go, but do not want to be confronted with the thought that it might be their destination.

Facing Death—and the Life After (1987)

Whatever clouds you face today, ask Jesus, the light of the world, to help you look behind the cloud to see His glory and His plans for you.

No matter what trials we face, Christ never leaves us. He is with us every step of the way!

Hope for Each Day (2006)

All around us are people who are lost and separated from their heavenly Father, and we have a responsibility to tell them about Him.

When our faith becomes nothing more than a series of rules and regulations, joy flees and our love for Christ grows cold.

The Journey (2006)

I never see important people—or anyone else—without having the deep realization that I am—first and foremost—an ambassador of the King of kings and Lord of lords. From the moment I enter the room, I am thinking about how I can get the conversation around to the Gospel.

If anything has been accomplished through my life, it has been solely God's doing, not mine, and He—not I—must get the credit.

Just as I Am (1997)

One of the greatest truths of the Bible is that God loves us. And because He loves us, He wants to give us what is best for us.

Sometimes we get tired of the burdens of life, but we know that Jesus Christ will meet us at the end of our life's journey—and that makes all the difference.

Answers to Life's Problems (1994)

To be sorry is not enough in repentance. Judas was sorry enough to hang himself. It was an admission of guilt without true repentance.

People have become so empty that they can't even entertain themselves. They have to pay other people to amuse them, to make them laugh, to try to make them feel warm and happy and comfortable for a few minutes.

Peace with God (1984)

Comfort and prosperity have never enriched the world as much as adversity has.

The Leadership Secrets of Billy Graham (2005)

Many invest wisely in business matters, but fail to invest time and interest in their most valued possessions: their spouses and children.

"Golden years" must have been coined by the young. It is doubtful that anyone over seventy would have described this phase of life with such a symbolic word.

Nearing Home: Life, Faith, and Finishing Well (2011)

Are you perhaps one of those who worries about having committed the unpardonable sin? If so, you should face squarely what the Bible says on this subject, not what you may have heard from others. The unpardonable sin is rejecting the truth about Christ. It is rejecting, completely and finally, the witness of the Holy Spirit, which declares that Jesus Christ is the Son of God who alone can save us from our sins. Have you rejected Christ in your own life, and said in your heart that what the Bible teaches about Him is a lie? Then I tell you as solemnly and as sincerely as I know how that you are in a very dangerous position.

All too often we are more afraid of physical pain than of moral wrong. The cross is the standing evidence of the fact that holiness is a principle for which God would die.

The Holy Spirit: Activating God's Power in Your Life (2000)

I have never known anyone to accept Christ's redemption and later regret it.

I will buy you back with My blood because I love you. I will free you from the chains of sin. I will settle the conflict within and give peace to your soul. But you must come to Me with a repentant heart. You must be willing to be redeemed. You must exchange your sin-blackened heart for a new heart that is cleansed by My blood.

The Reason for My Hope: Salvation (2013)

HALLEY, HENRY

Henry Halley was born in Kentucky in 1874. In 1924, after serving twenty-five years as a preacher, Henry produced the first edition of what would go on to become *Halley's Bible Handbook*. At the time, it was called *Suggestions for Bible Study* and was only sixteen pages long.

At first the Handbook was supported by donations and distributed for free. Only when printing costs became prohibitive did he begin charging for it. By 2007 *Halley's Bible Handbook* had sold more than five million copies in many languages.

Henry Halley's memory, combined with his continual Bible study, was such that he was reputed to be able to quote books of the Bible verbatim and could preach from memory for twenty-four hours at a time. He died in 1965 and was buried in Lexington, Kentucky.

☜

It is a glorious thing to be a Christian.

God Himself became a Man to give us a concrete, definite, tangible idea of what to think of when we think of God.

To run God's thoughts thru your mind often will make your mind grow like God's mind.

We believe the Bible to be, not man's account of his effort to find God, but rather an account of God's effort to reveal Himself to man.

The Bible is all One Story. The last part of the last book in the Bible reads like the close of the story begun in the first part of the first book.

What is there, what can there be, to make life worthwhile, apart from the Christian Hope?

Pocket Bible Handbook (1948)

HAVERGAL, FRANCES RIDLEY

With a clergyman and composer for a father, and a priest and organist for a brother, it was perhaps inevitable that Frances Ridley Havergal would become a hymn writer and author of religious poetry.

Born in 1836 in Worcestershire, England, Frances was an early reader, writing poetry by the time she was seven. She lived a short and quiet life, passing away at the young age of thirty-four. Though often plagued by poor health, she was an enthusiastic supporter of the Church Missionary Society. She has been described as a short-lived but bright candle in the history of English hymnody.

Hymns written by Frances Ridley Havergal include "Take My Life and Let It Be," "O Merciful Redeemer," and "Who Is on the Lord's Side?" Her poems have been compiled in the volumes *Poetical Works* and *Under His Shadow*.

✍

The very way in which we close a door or lay down a book may be a victory or a defeat, a witness to Christ's keeping or a witness that we are not truly being kept.

Compromising Christians are always weak Christians.

Literally, a consecrated life is and must be a life of denial of self.

Again and again God has shown that the influence of a very average life, when once really consecrated to Him, may outweigh that of almost any number of merely professing Christians.

There is nothing like singing [God's] own words. The preacher claims the promise, "My Word shall not return unto Me void," and why should not the singer equally claim it?

Unclaimed promises are like uncashed checks; they will keep us from bankruptcy, but not from want.

It is not so often a whole sermon as a single short sentence in it that wings God's arrow to a heart.

Kept for the Master's Use (1879)

Another year is dawning, dear Father, let it be
In working or in waiting, another year with Thee.

"Another Year Is Dawning" (1874)

Take my life, and let it be
Consecrated, Lord, to Thee.
Take my moments and my days;
Let them flow in ceaseless praise.

"Take My Life and Let It Be" (1874)

I gave My life for thee, My precious blood I shed,
That thou might ransomed be, and raised up from the dead.
I gave, I gave My life for thee, what hast thou given for Me?
I gave, I gave My life for thee, what hast thou given for Me?

"I Gave My Life for Thee" (1858)

Like a river glorious, is God's perfect peace,
Over all victorious, in its bright increase;
Perfect, yet it floweth, fuller every day,
Perfect, yet it groweth, deeper all the way.
Stayed upon Jehovah, hearts are fully blest
Finding, as He promised, perfect peace and rest.

"Like a River Glorious" hymn (1876)

HAYFORD, JACK

Born in 1934 in Los Angeles, California, Jack Williams Hayford is the founding pastor of The Church on the Way. In 1969 he took on the pastorship of a church with eighteen members. By 1980 The Church on the Way was a prototype megachurch. From 2004 to 2008 he served as president of the Foursquare Church, which teaches and celebrates the fourfold ministry of Christ: Savior, Baptizer (with the Holy Spirit), Healer, and coming King.

In addition to being a prolific author, he has written hundreds of hymns, including "Majesty," which has been listed in the top one hundred contemporary hymns sung worldwide.

His books include *Stepping Up in Faith*, *Daybreak: Walking Daily in Christ's Presence*, *Restoring Fallen Leaders*, *Praying for Those You Love*, and *Penetrating the Darkness: Discovering the Power of the Cross against Unseen Evil*.

The earliest blessing a child can receive from those influencing his or her life is to answer the question, How can I cultivate an atmosphere of God's order and love in our home and form an understanding mind-set that life is not to be lived for oneself but in the interest of others?

The children you and I can influence are more open to the things of the Spirit than adults often realize.

Blessing Your Children (2002)

God is seeking childlikeness in everyone; and there is something about the dependence of thirsting after righteousness and the simplicity of submitting to the Holy Spirit's supernatural work that humbles us all like children.

Jesus was everything of humanity and nothing of superficiality; everything of godliness and nothing of religiosity. Jesus ministered the joy, life, love and health—the glory—of His Kingdom, and He did it in the most practical, tasteful ways.

Glory on Your House (1991)

Nothing is more limiting than the self-imposed boundaries we clamp around our own lives when we require God to fit into our expectations.

Most of us don't pray on a regular basis because we're aware it will cost us something. . . . Honesty.

Prayer Is Invading the Impossible (2002)

There's a place in God's will for you, no matter what your age, no matter what your past.

The truth is, any major move or change in our lives can leave us disoriented and insecure. Oddly enough, however, it is in these very situations that you and I may encounter God as never before. These are the times to seek His face and His will with renewed intensity.

Pursuing the Will of God (1997)

The Holy Spirit, the third person of the Trinity—Father, Son, and Holy Spirit—is somewhat of a mystery to most people.

When a person comes to God the Father and willingly receives the gift of life through Jesus the Son, the first thing that happens is that the Holy Spirit enters that person's life. Jesus described Him as a "Comforter"— One who will remain beside you to help, to counsel, to teach, and to strengthen you.

Rebuilding the Real You: The Definitive Guide to the Holy Spirit's Work in Your Life (2009)

HENDRICKS, HOWARD

Born in 1924 in Philadelphia, Howard Hendricks was judged the boy most likely to end up in jail—until he met a teacher who refused to believe he wasn't better than that! He embraced the power of that belief, and in his more than fifty years as a professor at Dallas Theological Seminary, he applied it to his own students. Among the students who passed through his hermeneutics class were Chuck Swindoll, Tony Evans, Joseph Stowell, and David Jeremiah.

In 1986 the Dallas Theological Seminary opened the Howard G. Hendricks Center for Christian Leadership as a tribute to his life and work.

Howard passed away in Dallas in 2013.

His books include *Say It with Love, Heaven Help the Home, Taking a Stand: What God Can Do through Ordinary You,* and *Color Outside the Lines: A Revolutionary Approach to Creative Leadership.*

The home marks a child for life.

Children are not looking for perfect parents; but they are looking for honest parents.

Heaven Help the Home (1973)

Show me a man's closest companions and I can make a fairly accurate guess as to what sort of man he is, as well as what sort of man he is likely to become.

There is no substitute for knowing and being known by another human being.

As Iron Sharpens Iron (1995)

The greatest tragedy among Christians today is that too many of us are under the Word of God, but not in it for ourselves.

The genius of the Word of God is that it has staying power; it can stand up to repeated exposure. In fact, that's why it is unlike any other book. You may be an expert in a given field. If you read a book in that field two or three times you've got it. You can put it on the shelf and move on to something else. But that's never true of the Bible. Read it over and over again, and you'll see things that you've never seen before.

Living by the Book (1991)

Has it ever occurred to you that love is the greatest positive force in existence?

I find that the more love I show a person, the greater the impact I have on his life.

Say It with Love (1972)

HENRY, MATTHEW

Matthew Henry was born in 1662, the son of an English minister. His father was expelled from the church after refusing to accept the Act of Uniformity (a law prescribing the prayers and methods of worship to be used in church). He had enough of a private income to have his son trained as a lawyer, but Matthew chose to study theology instead.

He became a Presbyterian minister and is most famous for his written commentary of the entire Bible, a work that was praised by George Whitefield, Charles Spurgeon, and others. He lived until 1714.

He is the author of the *Exposition of the Old and New Testaments* (also known as the *Complete Commentary*). His other works, including sermons, were compiled as *The Miscellaneous Works of the Rev. Matthew Henry VDM*.

✍

An affliction rightly borne does us good.

A state of apostasy is worse than a state of ignorance.

Satan teaches men first to doubt and then to deny; he makes them skeptics first, and so by degrees makes them atheists.

In the word of God there is sweet and wholesome nourishment, milk for babies, honey for those that are grown up.

Whatever communion there is between our souls and Christ, it is He who begins the discourse.

Christ is not only beloved by all believing souls, but is their well-beloved, their best-beloved, their only beloved.

Our duty as Christians is always to keep heaven in our eye and the earth under our feet.

Ministers are the church's teeth; like nurses, they chew the meat for the babes of Christ.

Nothing is more injurious to the honor of the Eternal Mind than the supposition of eternal matter.

The beauty of believers consists in their resemblance to Jesus Christ.

Death to a good man, is his release from the imprisonment of this world, and his departure to the enjoyments of another world.

When God sends destruction on the ungodly, He commands deliverance for the righteous.

Those that keep themselves pure in times of common iniquity God will keep safe in times of common calamity.

We have a cunning adversary, who watches to do mischief, and will promote errors, even by the words of scripture.

Let us watch against unbelief, pride, and self-confidence. If we go forth in our own strength, we shall faint, and utterly fall; but having our hearts and our hopes in heaven, we shall be carried above all difficulties, and be enabled to lay hold of the prize of our high calling in Christ Jesus.

We best oppose error by promoting a solid knowledge of the word of truth; and the greatest kindness we can do to children, is to make them early to know the Bible.

Drunkenness is a sin that never goes alone, but carries men into other evils; it is a sin very provoking to God.

Envy is a sin that commonly carries with it its own punishment, in the rottenness of the bones.

It is very proper for friends, when they part, to part with prayer.

The bad will sooner debauch the good than the good reform the bad.

Which way soever a man's genius lies, he should endeavor to honor God and edify the church with it.

All created beings shrink to nothing in comparison with the Creator.

There is no resisting, nor escaping God's anger. See the mischief sin makes; it provokes God to anger. And those not humbled by lesser judgments, must expect greater.

Our way to heaven lies through the wilderness of this world.

Earth is embittered to us, that heaven may be endeared.

While the Lord is well-pleased in saving sinners through the righteousness of Christ, He will also glorify His justice by punishing all proud despisers.

There is as much danger from false brethren as from open enemies.

Nothing is pressed more earnestly in the scriptures than to walk as becomes those called to Christ's kingdom and glory.

He was made of the dust of the ground, a very unlikely thing to make man of; but the same infinite power that made the world of nothing made man, its masterpiece, of next to nothing. He was not made of gold-dust, powder of pearl, or diamond dust, but common dust, dust of the ground. Our fabric is earthly, and the fashioning of it like that of an earthen vessel. What have we then to be proud of?

A gracious soul can reconcile itself to the poorest accommodations; if it may have communication with God in them.

Never was any love lost that was bestowed upon Christ.

We have no joy but in Christ.

Were we to think more of our own mistakes and offences, we should be less apt to judge other people.

None are ruined by the justice of God but those that hate to be reformed by the grace of God.

The law sets before us our wretched state by sin, but there it leaves us. It discovers our disease, but does not make known the cure.

Many such there have been, and are, who speak lightly of the restraints of God's law, and deem themselves freed from obligations to obey it. Let Christians stand at a distance from such.

Let us seek to have our minds prepared for receiving things hard to be understood, by putting in practice things which are more easy to be understood.

Those who deceive others, deceive themselves, as they will find at last, to their cost.

The blood of the martyrs, though not a sacrifice of atonement, yet was a sacrifice of acknowledgment to the grace of God and His truth.

The blood of the martyrs has been the seed of the church.

The mind of man is a busy thing; if it is not employed in doing good, it will be doing evil.

We have no reason to expect pardon, except we seek it by faith in Christ; and that is always attended by true repentance, and followed by newness of life, by hatred of sin, and love to God.

When we are calling to God to turn the eye of His favor towards us He is calling to us to turn the eye of our obedience towards Him.

The waters which broke down everything else bore up the ark. The more the waters increased the higher the ark was lifted up towards heaven.

It is easy to be religious when religion is in fashion; but it is an evidence of strong faith and resolution to swim against a stream to heaven, and to appear for God when no one else appears for him.

The spring would not be so pleasant as it is if it did not succeed the winter.

Thy praying voice is music in God's ears.

Pride and self-conceit are sins that beset great men. They are apt to take that glory to themselves which is due to God only.

We should take heed of pride; it is a sin that turned angels into devils.

He that feeds His birds will not starve His babes.

Regeneration, or the new birth, is a subject to which the world is very averse; it is, however, the grand concern, in comparison with which everything else is but trifling.

When men do not fear God, they will not regard man.

Saints are often drowsy, and listless, and half asleep; but the word and Spirit of Christ will put life and vigor into the soul.

God will reward even the meanest drudgery done from a sense of duty, and with a view to glorify Him.

The ordinances of Christ are the ornaments of the Church.

While the necessity of a holy walk is insisted upon, as the effect and evidence of the knowledge of God in Christ Jesus, the opposite error of self-righteous pride is guarded against with equal care.

All sin must be wept over; here, in godly sorrow, or, hereafter, in eternal misery.

Dare we make light of that which brings down the wrath of God?

The way of sin is downhill; a man cannot stop himself when he will. Suppress the first emotions of sin, and leave it off before it be meddled with.

Sinners are pleased with gods that neither see, nor hear, nor know; but they will be judged by One to whom all things are open.

When wickedness has become general then universal ruin is not far off; while there is a remnant of praying people in a nation, to empty the measure as it fills, judgments may be kept off a great while.

The body is but a tabernacle, or tent, of the soul.

What does it signify though we are well able to act our parts in life, in every other respect, if at last we hear from the Supreme Judge, "Depart from me, I know you not, ye workers of iniquity?"

Those that would not eat the forbidden fruit must not come near the forbidden tree.

Good Christians will be afraid of giving any occasion to those about them to question their faith in Christ and their love to him.

Christ is the center of the church's unity.

When we take God for our God we must take His people for our people in all conditions.

The woman was made of a rib out of the side of Adam; not made out of his head to rule over him, nor out of his feet to be trampled upon by him, but out of his side to be equal with him, under his arm to be protected, and near his heart to be beloved.

If man is the head, she is the crown, a crown to her husband, the crown of the visible creation. The man was dust refined, but the woman was dust double-refined, one remove further from the earth.

Matthew Henry's Commentary on the Whole Bible (1706)

HYBELS, BILL

Born in Michigan in 1952, Bill Hybels was heading toward a career in business when a lecture on Acts 2–style churches led him in a different direction. Shortly afterward he and a few friends started a church youth group. As they sought to make the teaching relevant while remaining true to the Bible, they saw their membership skyrocket.

Four years later he started a new church in an old theater building. First, he and his colleagues surveyed the area to find out why people weren't attending church. Addressing those questions helped make the church a success, and Willow Creek went on to become a prototype megachurch. It is regularly listed as one of the most influential churches in America.

His books include *Authenticity: Being Honest with God and Others*, *Essential Christianity: Practical Steps for Spiritual Growth*, and *The Power of a Whisper: Hearing God and Having the Guts to Respond*.

✍

Our minds, like the needle in that compass, can focus on a variety of subjects throughout the day. But in the end, when they're left alone to settle, they'll focus on the objects of our greatest affection.

When we're enjoying a right relationship with God and a right relationship with our parents, we have the most important relationships in life in order—and the freedom to establish a right relationship with the world.

Laws of the Heart (1985)

These days, I'm more convinced than ever that the absolute highest value in personal evangelism is staying attuned to and cooperative with the Holy Spirit.

You don't have to be any more talented, any richer, any slimmer, any smarter, any more or less of anything to partner with God. All you have to be is willing to be used by him in everyday ways.

Just Walk Across the Room (2006)

Can you imagine what would happen if each husband said, "My wife is a very important person, and I am going to honor, respect and encourage her." And if the wife said the same thing about her husband?

Obedience means taking action—to love one another, to restore a relationship, to confront a person in sin.

Descending into Greatness (1993)

Someone has said that when we work, we work; but when we pray, God works. His supernatural strength is available to praying people who are convinced to the core of their beings that He can make a difference.

A "prayer warrior" is a person who is convinced that God is omnipotent—that God has the power to do anything, to change anyone and to intervene in any circumstance. A person who truly believes this refuses to doubt God.

Too Busy Not to Pray (1988)

He knows that unless we honor Him as our ultimate need-meeter, we will entrust our needs to fallible humans who will be unable to meet them.

God's promises of joy and peace and satisfaction are not made just to married people.

Fit to Be Tied: Making Marriage Last a Lifetime (1991)

JEREMIAH, DAVID

Forty years after his birth in 1941 in Toledo, Ohio, Dr. David Jeremiah became senior pastor of Shadow Mountains Community Church. The following year he founded his Turning Point ministry to preach the "unchanging word of God in an ever-changing world."

His daily radio program, *The David Jeremiah Difference*, is shared with over two thousand stations across the world. The ministry's 2010 Going Global program aimed to translate Dr. Jeremiah's messages into the world's top twenty-five languages in an attempt to "be witnesses. . .to the ends of the earth."

He is author or coauthor of twenty-nine books, including *Sanctuary: Finding Moments of Refuge in the Presence of God*, *Captured by Grace: No One Is Beyond the Reach of a Loving God*, and *I Never Thought I'd See the Day: Culture at the Crossroads*.

✍

It is possible to live the Christian life just on the surface, knowing only enough to carry on an intelligent conversation in the church foyer with another equally uninformed believer. But when that happens you are vulnerable to the attack of the deceiver.

For all his power, Satan is neither omnipotent, omniscient, nor omnipresent. His power has limitations, and he can only act within the limits imposed upon him by God. God is greater than Satan and his evil, which will never be able to separate Christians from God's love.

Spiritual Warfare (1995)

Evil is not abstract. An intelligent being is the source of evil, and he assigns the administration of his works to real angelic creatures.

Men are not sent to hell because of being murderers or liars, they are sent to hell because they are unrighteous.

Escape the Coming Night (1990)

We are being given the opportunity to be firsthand observers to the staging of events that will precede the ultimate coming of Christ to this earth. Events written centuries ago are now unfolding right before our eyes and are telling us that our patient anticipation will soon be rewarded.

What would you like to be doing when [Jesus] returns? Where would you like to be when the trumpet sounds, when the archangel shouts, and when, in the twinkling of an eye, we are changed and rise into the clouds to meet Him?

What in the World Is Going On? (2008)

It is possible to be at the top of Christian service, respected and admired, and not have that indispensable ingredient by which God has chosen to work in His world today—the absolute sacrificial agape love of the Eternal God.

The Bible says that love is a responsibility. We are commanded to love. God doesn't ask us if we feel like it, He tells us in His Word that it is our responsibility to love.

The Power of Love (1994)

The very thing that most qualifies us to pray is our helplessness.

Answers to prayer have to be on God's schedule, not ours. He hears us pray, and He answers according to His will in His own time.

The Prayer Matrix (2004)

Above all else, He loves you and chose to measure that love out not in words, but in blood. He loves you enough to give you the greatest gift conceivable. Would such a love allow you to suffer without purpose?

He doesn't exult in your pain, but He delights in your tighter embrace.

A Bend in the Road (2000)

JOHN OF THE CROSS

John of the Cross (Juan de la Cruz) was a Spanish mystic and Carmelite friar who was proclaimed a saint 135 years after his death in 1591 at the age of forty-nine. His writings on faith and the soul led to his becoming one of the thirty-five Doctors of the Catholic Church—thinkers on theology whose work helped shape the modern church.

Salvador Dali's painting *Christ of Saint John of the Cross* was inspired by a charcoal sketch John made of the crucifixion.

In addition to a large body of poetry, John of the Cross also wrote *The Ascent of Mount Carmel* and *Sayings of Light and Love*.

✍

At a certain point in the spiritual journey God will draw a person from the beginning stage to a more advanced stage. . . . Such souls will likely experience what is called "the dark night of the soul." The "dark night" is when those persons lose all the pleasure that they once experienced in their devotional life. This happens because God wants to purify them and move them on to greater heights.

God perceives the imperfections within us, and because of His love for us, urges us to grow up. His love is not content to leave us in our weakness, and for this reason He takes us into a dark night. He weans us from all of the pleasures by giving us dry times and inward darkness.

Through the dark night pride becomes humility, greed becomes simplicity, wrath becomes contentment, luxury becomes peace, gluttony becomes moderation, envy becomes joy, and sloth becomes strength.

A soul will never grow until it is able to let go of the tight grasp it has on God.

The truth is that the feelings we receive from our devotional life are the least of its benefits. The invisible and unfelt grace of God is much greater, and it is beyond our comprehension.

Selected Writings (16th century)

JULIAN OF NORWICH

Born in 1342 in Norfolk, England, Julian of Norwich was an anchoress (a woman who has withdrawn from the world to concentrate on religious devotions). Little is known about her personally, and even the name "Julian" was probably taken from the church where she lived rather than being her own. Her writings, however, have been widely read and are respected across many denominations.

At a time when she was thought to be on her deathbed, she experienced several visions of Christ. Recovering, she wrote about them—and went on to live another forty years, passing away in 1416 in Norwich, England.

She wrote *Revelations of Divine Love* (also known as *The Short Text*) and *Showing of Love* (also known as *The Long Text*).

✍

He is to us everything which is good and comforting for our help. He is our clothing who wraps and enfolds us for love, embraces us and shelters us, surrounds us for His love which is so tender that He may never desert us.

God is the Creator and the protector and the lover. For until I am substantially united to Him, I can never have perfect rest or true happiness, until, that is, I am so attached to Him that there can be no created thing between my God and me.

It is very greatly pleasing to Him that a simple soul should come naked, openly, and familiarly.

We are so preciously loved by God that we cannot even comprehend it. No created being can ever know how much and how sweetly and tenderly God loves them. It is only with the help of His grace that we are able to persevere in spiritual contemplation with endless wonder at His high, surpassing, immeasurable love which our Lord in His goodness has for us.

The highest form of prayer is to the goodness of God. It comes down to us to meet our humblest needs. It gives life to our souls and makes them live and grow in grace and virtue.

Revelations of Divine Love (14th century)

KENNEDY, D. JAMES

Born in Georgia in 1930, Dennis James Kennedy was an American pastor, evangelist, and broadcaster. At the age of twenty-nine he was ordained and became pastor of Coral Ridge Presbyterian Church. He preached at Coral Ridge for the next forty-seven years, until his death in 2007.

Having been brought to faith by a radio preacher, D. James Kennedy also preached his faith through radio and television. He presented *Truth That Transforms* on radio and *The Coral Ridge Hour* on television. He was a founding member of the Moral Majority in 1979 and was inducted in the National Religious Broadcasters' Hall of Fame in 2003.

His books include *The Da Vinci Myth versus Gospel Truth* and *What If Jesus Had Never Been Born?*

✍

It is not because of any want of historical data that people do not believe the scripture or do not believe in Christ. Rather, it is because of a want of a moral disposition to surrender one's life to the Lordship and authority of Jesus Christ.

It doesn't matter if everyone in the world joins hands and votes unanimously that God's truth is false, it still remains true. It remains true whether I believe in it or I don't believe in it.

Why I Believe (1980)

Not only did all the early Christians witness, but they witnessed daily and to everyone they met—especially to those who were in their network of friends, relatives, associates, and neighbors.

Evangelism Explosion (1996)

Atheism is so senseless. When I look at the solar system, I see the earth at the right distance from the sun to receive the proper amounts of light and heat. This did not happen by chance.

What If Jesus Had Never Been Born? (1994)

William Law, born in 1686, was a Church of England priest at a turbulent time. Queen Anne, the last of the Stuart dynasty, had died, and the British throne had been given to Protestant George of Hanover even though many (Catholic) Stuarts had better claims. His refusal to abandon his allegiance to the Stuarts led to his steady demotion through the church ranks.

When he could no longer preach as a priest, he taught privately and wrote extensively. His principled stance and his writings influenced many, both in his lifetime and afterward. He died in 1761 in the same town in which he was born.

His written works include *A Serious Call to a Devout and Holy Life*, *The Spirit of Love*, *A Dialogue between a Methodist and a Churchman*, and *An Humble and Earnest Address to the Clergy* (also known as *The Power of the Spirit*).

☜

Unless the common course of our lives be according to the common spirit of our prayers, our prayers are so far from being a real or sufficient degree of devotion that they become an empty lip-labor, or, what is worse, a notorious hypocrisy.

For who does not know, that it is better to be pure and holy, than to talk about purity and holiness?

For as thankfulness is an express acknowledgement of the goodness of God towards you, so repining and complaints are as plain accusations of want of God's goodness towards you.

Will you let the fear of a false world, that has no love for you, keep you from the fear of that God, who has only created you, that he may love and bless you to all eternity?

If anyone would tell you the surest, shortest way to all happiness and all perfection, he must tell you to make it a rule to yourself, to thank God for everything that happens to you.

A Serious Call to a Devout and Holy Life (1729)

It is the same impossibility for a thing to be created out of nothing, as to be created by nothing.

An Appeal to All That Doubt (c. 1730)

Choose any life but the life of God and heaven, and you choose death, for death is nothing else but the loss of the life of God.

Since Christ has an infinite power, and also an infinite desire to save mankind, how can anyone miss of this salvation, but through his own unwillingness to be saved by Him?

Awake, thou that sleepest, and Christ, who from all eternity hath been espoused to thy soul, shall give thee light.

Pride, self-exaltation, hatred, and persecution, under a cloak of religious zeal, will sanctify actions which nature, left to itself, would be ashamed to own.

Long for nothing, desire nothing, hope for nothing, but to have all that is within thee changed into the spirit and holy temper of the holy Jesus. Let this be thy Christianity, thy church, and thy religion.

Depart in the least degree from the goodness of God, and you depart into evil, because nothing is good but His goodness.

God, the only good of all intelligent natures, is not an absent or distant God, but is more present in and to our souls, than our own bodies.

For the sun meets not the springing bud that stretches towards him, with half that certainty, as God, the source of all good, communicates Himself to the soul that longs to partake of Him.

The goodness of God breaking forth into a desire to communicate good, was the cause and the beginning of the creation.

Heaven is as near to our souls, as this world is to our bodies; and we are created, we are redeemed, to have our conversation in it.

We starve in the midst of plenty, groan under infirmities, with the remedy in our own hands.

The Spirit of Prayer (1823)

Wherever pride is, there the devil is riding in his first fiery chariot.

Love, goodness, and communication of good is the immutable glory and perfection of the divine nature, and nothing can have union with God, but that which partakes of this goodness.

The love that brought forth the existence of all things, changes not through the fall of its creatures, but is continually at work, to bring back all fallen nature and creature to their first state of goodness.

The highest angel has nothing of its own that it can offer unto God, no more light, love, purity, perfection, and glorious hallelujahs, that spring from itself, or its own powers, than the poorest creature upon earth.

Divine inspiration was essential to man's first created state. The Spirit of the triune God, breathed into, or brought to life in him, was that alone which made him a holy creature in the image and likeness of God.

For the creature's true religion, is its rendering to God all that is God's, it is its true continual acknowledging all that which it is, and has, and enjoys, in and from God.

The Spirit of God first gives, or sows the seed of divine union in the soul of every man; and religion is that by which it is quickened, raised, and brought forth to a fullness and growth of a life in God.

A religious faith that is uninspired, a hope, or love that proceeds not from the immediate working of the divine nature within us, can no more do any divine good to our souls, or unite them with the goodness of God, than an hunger after earthly food can feed us with the immortal bread of heaven.

I appeal to every man, whether popish and Protestant churches need do anything else, than that which they now do, and have done for ages, to prove their faithfulness to such a master, and their full obedience to His precepts.

To make men kill men, is meat and drink to that roaring adversary of mankind, who goeth about seeking whom he may devour.

An Humble, Affectionate, and Earnest Address (1761)

Lewis, C. S.

Born in Belfast, Ireland, in 1898, Clive Staples (or Jack) Lewis was a man of many interests, being a novelist, poet, academic, medievalist, literary critic, essayist, lay theologian, and Christian apologist.

He was baptized in the Church of Ireland but followed the seemingly traditional route of becoming an atheist in his teenage years. In his thirties the influence of J. R. R. Tolkien (with whom he taught English at Oxford University) and the writings of George MacDonald and G. K. Chesterton brought him back into the Anglican Communion, and he joined the Church of England.

His radio talks during World War II were credited with being great boosters of the public morale.

He died on the same day John F. Kennedy was assassinated.

He is the author of *The Chronicles of Narnia*, *The Screwtape Letters*, *Surprised by Joy*, *The Four Loves*, and many other works.

Those who put themselves in His hands will become perfect, as He is perfect—perfect in love, wisdom, joy, beauty, and immortality. The change will not be completed in this life, for death is an important part of the treatment.

In God's dimension, so to speak, you find a being who is three Persons while remaining one Being, just as a cube is six squares while remaining one cube.

Mere Christianity (1952)

A spoiled saint, a Pharisee, an inquisitor, or a magician, makes better sport in Hell than a mere common tyrant or debauchee.

Catch [a man] at the moment when he is really poor in spirit and smuggle into his mind the gratifying reflection, "By jove! I'm being humble," and almost immediately pride—pride at his own humility—will appear.

The Screwtape Letters (1941)

Everyone feels benevolent if nothing happens to be annoying him at the moment.

God whispers to us in our pleasures, speaks in our conscience, but shouts in our pains.

The Problem of Pain (1947)

I do not believe one can settle how much we ought to give. I am afraid the only safe rule is to give more than we can spare.

The limit of giving is to be the limit of our ability to give.

Words to Live By (c. 1940)

The humiliation leads to a greater glory.

I believe in Christianity as I believe the Sun has risen, not only because I see it, but because by it I see everything else.

The Weight of Glory (1949)

I need Christ, not something that resembles Him.

You never know how much you really believe anything until its truth or falsehood becomes a matter of life and death to you.

A Grief Observed (1961)

Heaven is not a state of mind. Heaven is reality itself.

There are only two kinds of people in the end: those who say to God, "Thy will be done," and those to whom God says, in the end, "Thy will be done." All that are in hell, choose it. Without that self-choice there could be no hell. No soul that seriously and constantly desires joy will ever miss it. Those who seek find. To those who knock it is opened.

The Great Divorce (1946)

Friendship is born at that moment when one man says to another: "What! You too? I thought that no one but myself. .."

To love at all is to be vulnerable. Love anything and your heart will be wrung and possibly broken. If you want to make sure of keeping it intact you must give it to no one, not even an animal. Wrap it carefully round with hobbies and little luxuries; avoid all entanglements. Lock it up safe in the casket or coffin of your selfishness. But in that casket, safe, dark, motionless, airless, it will change. It will not be broken; it will become unbreakable, impenetrable, irredeemable. To love is to be vulnerable.

The Four Loves (1960)

LLOYD-JONES, D. MARTYN

Born in 1899 to a Welsh grocer, David Martyn Lloyd-Jones studied medicine in London and worked as an assistant to the Royal Physician. Before long, however, he felt the call to ministry and preached in Wales for ten years before returning to London as associate pastor of Westminster Chapel. He eventually became sole pastor of the Congregationalist church and led it into the Fellowship of Independent Evangelical Churches.

He was opposed to the "broad church" attitude and encouraged many evangelicals to leave churches that seemed to be taking too liberal an approach.

He died in 1981 in Ealing, England.

His written works include *Why Does God Allow War?*, *Truth Unchanged, Unchanging*, and *The Plight of Man and the Power of God*. Over sixteen hundred of his sermons are also available in audio recordings.

The power of the devil is, after all, nothing but a usurped power.

All man's troubles emanate from his pride.

The Cross (1986)

Take the Ten Commandments, for instance. People joke about them, do they not? They even make films of them. They do everything but keep them!

The first great characteristic of the true Christian is always a sense of thankfulness and of gratitude to God.

Love So Amazing (1962)

If I had no other reason for believing this book called the Bible, I would believe it for this reason: it is the only book I know of that tells me the plain, unvarnished truth about myself—the only one.

If you have not seen your utter, absolute need of being forgiven by God and being reconciled to Him, then your whole position is wrong, and you have no right to consider anything else.

Compelling Christianity (2007)

LOTZ, ANNE GRAHAM

Anne Graham Lotz, who was born in 1948 in Montreat, North Carolina, is the daughter of Billy and Ruth Graham. Despite some conservative objections to the idea of a female evangelist, she is considered to be one of the top five evangelists in America.

In 1988 she founded AnGeL Ministries—whose name is based on her initials and the idea that angels are messengers of God, as she was attempting to be—and began teaching in countries across the world.

A time of intense personal trial led to a change in direction. Her "Just Give Me Jesus" meetings, which have been held in twelve countries, stress and encourage spiritual revival among women.

In addition to her *Daily Light for Daily Living* radio broadcasts, she has authored several books, including *Just Give Me Jesus*, *Trusting God When You Don't Understand*, and *A Wake-Up Call for God's People*.

✍

In their pride, the builders of Babel assumed they could work their way into God's Presence and He would accept them on the basis of what they had done. They were wrong then, and they are still wrong today.

Whose advice are you taking and whose example are you watching?

God's Story (1997)

If our lives are easy, and if all we ever attempt for God is what we know we can handle, how will we ever experience His omnipotence in our lives?

Our love for Christ is more important to Him than all of our service to Him. Strict obedience and service alone are not enough. Love for Jesus must come first.

The Vision of His Glory (1996)

Like a rose whose fragrance is sweetest when its petals are crushed, the fragrance of Christ is made sweeter in our lives by affliction.

No storm is so great, no wave is so high, no sea is so deep, no wind is so strong, that Jesus cannot either calm it or carry us through it.

The Daily Light Journal (2004)

Reject low living, sight walking, small planning, casual praying, and limited giving—God has chosen you for greatness.

Do you sometimes feel that you just can't take one more thing? Even in your misery, be mindful that the very weight of your burdens and the intensity of the pressure may be exactly what God is going to use in your life to trigger an experience of personal revival.

I Saw the Lord (2006)

Before the foundation of the world was laid, God, in His divine sovereignty, planned to send His own Son to the cross to be our Savior.

One way to drive Satan to distraction, and to overcome him, is through praise of Jesus.

Just Give Me Jesus (2002)

Five minutes before you see Jesus face to face, what will you wish you had done differently. . .today? Do it!

No One Knows about That Day (2009)

Make no mistake about it! Heaven is a home populated by the Lord and His loved ones who have made the deliberate choice to be there.

Based on your choices you have made, if you were to die today, would you be inside or outside of Heaven's gates?

Heaven, My Father's House (2002)

"But, Lord. . ." is an oxymoron, isn't it? It's a contradiction in terms, because if Jesus is Lord, then we say, "Yes, Sir," not, "But, Lord."

The kind of trust God wants us to have cannot be learned in comfort and ease.

Why? Trusting God When You Don't Understand (2004)

LUCADO, MAX

Born in San Angelo, Texas, in 1955, Max Lucado went to Abilene Christian University intending to become a lawyer, but a required Bible course that included a mandatory mission trip turned his life around. Later, while working as an associate minister at a church in Miami, he wrote a regular column for the church's newsletter. That experience developed a talent for writing that would take his message all over the world.

After working twenty years as pastor at Oak Hills Church, health problems forced him to step down. He later resumed work with a copastor.

Christianity Today has called him "America's Pastor."

He has published nearly one hundred books, including *What the Cross Means to Me, A Heart Like Jesus, God Thinks You're Wonderful,* and *Facing Your Giants.*

God's blessings are dispersed according to the riches of his grace, not according to the depth of our faith.

The best of Satan melts as wax before the presence of Christ.

A Gentle Thunder (1995)

The lack of God-centeredness leads to self-centeredness. Sin celebrates its middle letter—sIn.

Where we might think of sin as slip-ups or missteps, God views sin as a godless attitude that leads to godless actions.

Come Thirsty (2004)

How grimy did God get when He reached down to clean you up? How grimy are you willing to get in order to be an "imitator of God"?

Are you in a dilemma, wondering if you should tell the truth or not? The question to ask in such moments is, Will God bless my deceit? Will He, who hates lies, bless a strategy built on lies? Will the Lord, who loves the truth, bless the business of falsehoods?

Just Like Jesus (1998)

When our deepest desire is not the things of God, or a favor from God, but God Himself, we cross a threshold.

Your pain has a purpose. Your problems, struggles, heartaches, and hassles cooperate toward one end—the glory of God.

It's Not about Me (2004)

The soldiers gasped. Saul sighed. Goliath jeered. David swung. And God made His point. "Anyone who underestimates what God can do with the ordinary has rocks in his head."

Being a parent is better than a course on theology. Being a father is teaching me that when I am criticized, injured, or afraid, there is a Father who is ready to comfort me.

The Applause of Heaven (1990)

When you're full of yourself, God can't fill you. But when you empty yourself, God has a useful vessel.

We exist to exhibit God, to display His glory. We serve as canvases for His brush stroke, papers for His pen, soil for His seeds, glimpses of His image.

Cure for the Common Life (2005)

If God can make a billion galaxies, can't He make good out of our bad and sense out of our faltering lives? Of course He can. He is God.

God handles the task, start to finish.

3:16: The Numbers of Hope (2007)

You see, it's one thing to accept Him as Lord, another to recognize Him as Savior—but it's another matter entirely to accept Him as Father.

It's easy to forget who is the servant and who is to be served.

He Still Moves Stones (1993)

We face death, but thanks to Jesus, we only face its shadow.

Don't measure the size of the mountain; talk to the One who can move it.

Traveling Light (2001)

When you recognize God as Creator, you will admire Him. When you recognize His wisdom, you will learn from Him. When you discover His strength, you will rely on Him. But only when He saves you will you worship Him.

Worship is a voluntary act of gratitude offered by the saved to the Savior, by the healed to the Healer, and by the delivered to the Deliverer.

In the Eye of the Storm (1991)

There is something about keeping Him divine that keeps Him distant, packaged, predictable. But don't do it. For heaven's sake, don't. Let Him be as human as He intended to be. Let Him into the mire and muck of our world. For only if we let Him in can He pull us out.

Among the voices that found their way into the carpentry shop in Nazareth was your voice. Your silent prayers uttered on tearstained pillows were heard before they were said. Your deepest questions about death and eternity were answered before they were asked. And your direst need for a Savior was met before you ever sinned.

God Came Near (1986)

Sin has sired a thousand heartaches and broken a million promises. Your addiction can be traced back to sin. Your mistrust can be traced back to sin. Bigotry, robbery, adultery—all because of sin. But in heaven, all of this will end.

We are so good at waiting that we don't wait forwardly. We forget to look. We are so patient that we become complacent. We are too content. We seldom search the skies. We rarely run to the temple. We seldom, if ever, allow the Holy Spirit to interrupt our plans and lead us to worship so that we might see Jesus.

When Christ Comes (1999)

Do you understand what God has done? He has deposited a Christ seed in you. As it grows, you will change. It's not that sin has no more presence in your life, but rather that sin has no more power over your life.

Jesus' survival weapon of choice is scripture. If the Bible was enough for His wilderness, shouldn't it be enough for yours?

Next-Door Savior (2003)

Condemnation—the preferred commodity of Satan.

Behold the fruit of grace: saved by God, raised by God, seated with God. Gifted, equipped, and commissioned.

Grace (2012)

God will use your mess for good. We see a perfect mess; God sees a perfect chance to train, test, and teach.

You represent a challenge to Satan's plan. You carry something of God within you, something noble and holy, something the world needs—wisdom, kindness, mercy, skill. If Satan can neutralize you, he can mute your influence.

You'll Get through This: Hope and Help for Your Turbulent Times (2013)

Seek first the kingdom of wealth and you'll worry over every dollar. Seek first the kingdom of health and you'll sweat every blemish and bump. Seek first the kingdom of popularity, and you'll relive every conflict. Seek first the kingdom of safety, and you'll jump at every crack of the twig. But seek first His kingdom and you will find it. On that, we can depend and never worry.

As followers of God, you and I have a huge asset. We know everything is going to turn out all right. God hasn't budged from His throne.

Fearless (2012)

Deliverance is to the Bible what jazz music is to Mardi Gras—bold, brassy, and everywhere.

He saw you, picked you, and placed you. "You did not choose me; I chose you" (John 15:16). Before you are a butcher, baker, or cabinetmaker; male or female; Asian or black, you are God's child. Replacement or fill-in? Hardly. You are God's first choice.

God Will Carry You Through (2013)

Bread of Life? Jesus lived up to the title. But an unopened loaf does a person no good. Have you received the bread? Have you received God's forgiveness?

Outlive Your Life: You Were Made to Make a Difference (2010)

Grace is everything Jesus. Grace lives because He does, works because He works, and matters because He matters.

The resurrection of Jesus will not lose its power. The blood of Christ will not fade in strength. God never changes. You can count on it.

One God, One Plan, One Life (2013)

God occupies the only seat on the supreme court of heaven. He wears the robe and refuses to share the gavel.

Forgiveness is not foolishness. Forgiveness is, at its core, choosing to see your offender with different eyes.

Facing Your Giants (2006)

When a person becomes a follower of Christ, when sins are confessed and the grace of Jesus is accepted, a wonderful miracle of the soul occurs. The person is placed "in" Christ.

God has only one requirement for entrance into heaven: that we be clothed in Christ.

Beyond Heaven's Door (2013)

Today. This day. In the stink of it. The throes of it, Jesus makes a miracle out of it. When others nail you to the cross of your past, He swings open the door to your future. Paradise. Jesus treats your shame-filled days with grace.

Need spice in your day? Thank God for every problem that comes down the pike. Is any situation so dire that gratitude is eliminated?

Great Every Day (2012)

Guilt is not what God wants for His children. When repentance occurs in the heart of the believer, forgiveness is extended by the Father.

God's love is eternal. You are always on God's itinerary. Come and go as you wish, but He's always there.

Max on Life: Answers and Insights to Your Most Important Questions (2011)

Have you ever wondered why God gives so much? We could exist on far less. He could have left the world flat and gray; we wouldn't have known the difference. But He didn't.

God's gifts shed light on God's heart, God's good and generous heart.

He Chose the Nails (2012)

The first step in understanding the Bible is asking God to help us. We should read prayerfully. If anyone understands God's Word, it is because of God and not the reader.

Before reading the Bible, pray. Invite God to speak to you. Don't go to scripture looking for your idea, go searching for His.

Life Lessons: Book of James (2007)

LUTHER, MARTIN

Martin Luther, born in 1483 in Eisleben, Saxony, was a German priest who objected to the practice of "indulgences" current at the time. The notion that God's forgiveness could be bought appalled him. But his stance brought him into conflict with vested interests within the Roman Catholic Church.

He believed the established priesthood was not the only channel to God for the ordinary worshipper and taught that each baptized Christian had a direct link with God. He translated the Bible into the common tongue, further reducing the people's dependence on the established priesthood.

Arguably the preeminent influence in the Protestant Reformation of the sixteenth century, he lived until 1546.

In addition to translating the Bible, he also wrote *Table Talks* and many exegetical works sometimes compiled as *The Erlangen Edition*, *The Weimar Edition*, or *The American Edition*.

There is no greater anger than when God is silent, and talks not with us, but suffers us to go on in our sinful works, and to do all things according to our own passions and pleasure.

Better it were that God should be angry with us, than that we be angry with God, for He can soon be at an union with us again, because He is merciful; but when we are angry with Him, then the case is not to be helped.

Let us not flutter too high, but remain by the manger and the swaddling-clothes of Christ.

Let whatsoever will or can befall me, I will surely cleave by my sweet Savior Christ Jesus, for in Him am I baptized; I can neither do nor know anything but only what He has taught me.

Infinite potentates have raged against this book, and sought to destroy and uproot it—king Alexander the Great, the princes of Egypt and of Babylon, the monarchs of Persia, of Greece, and of Rome, the emperors Julius and Augustus—but they nothing prevailed; they are all gone and vanished, while the book remains.

The holy scripture is the highest and best of books, abounding in comfort under all afflictions and trials.

We ought not to criticize, explain, or judge the scriptures by our mere reason, but diligently, with prayer, meditate thereon, and seek their meaning.

Let us not lose the Bible, but with diligence, in fear and invocation of God, read and preach it.

The Bible is the book that makes fools of the wise of this world; it is only understood by the plain and simple hearted.

Esteem this book as the precious fountain that can never be exhausted.

In it thou findest the swaddling-clothes and the manger whither the angels directed the poor, simple shepherds; they seem poor and mean, but dear and precious is the treasure that lies therein.

The holy scripture of itself is certain and true; God grant me grace to catch hold of its just use.

Let [God], for ever so short a while, keep back the sun, so that it shine not, or lock up air, water, or fire, ah! how willingly would we give all our wealth to have the use of these creatures again.

The kingdom of Christ is a kingdom of grace, mercy, and of all comfort.

Christ desires nothing more of us than that we speak of Him.

I know no other Christ than He who was crucified, and who in His Word is pictured and presented unto me.

We should consider the histories of Christ three manner of ways; first, as a history of acts or legends; secondly, as a gift or a present; thirdly, as an example, which we should believe and follow.

God deals with godly Christians much as with the ungodly, yea, and sometimes far worse.

God very wonderfully entrusts his highest office to preachers that are themselves poor sinners who, while teaching it, very weakly follow it.

In the beginning, God made Adam out of a piece of clay, and Eve out of Adam's rib: He blessed them and said: "Be fruitful and increase"—words that will stand and remain powerful to the world's end.

The thanks the world now gives to the doctrine of the gospel, is the same it gave to Christ, namely, the cross; 'tis what we must expect.

No man understands the scriptures, unless he be acquainted with the cross.

How many sorts of deaths are in our bodies? Nothing is therein but death.

We should always be ready when God knocks, prepared to take our leave of this world like Christians.

Such fair and glorious colors do the ungodly ever bear in this world, while in truth and deed they are condemners, scoffers, and rebels to the Word of God.

The devil and temptations also afford us occasion to learn and understand the scriptures, by experience and practice.

He that believes God's Word overcomes all, and remains secure everlastingly, against all misfortunes; for this shield fears nothing, neither hell nor the devil.

Thus is the devil ever God's ape.

The devil can affright, murder, and steal; but God revives and comforts.

God scorns and mocks the devil, in setting under his very nose a poor, weak, human creature, mere dust and ashes, yet endowed with the firstfruits of the Spirit, against whom the devil can do nothing.

We cannot vex the devil more than by teaching, preaching, singing, and talking of Jesus.

The Lord said to Christ: "Rule in the midst of thine enemies." On the other hand, the devil claims to be prince and God of the world.

'Tis impossible for Jesus Christ and the devil ever to remain under the same roof. The one must yield to the other—the devil to Christ.

The wrath is fierce and devouring which the devil has against the Son of God, and against mankind.

The devil assaults the Christian world with highest power and subtlety, vexing true Christians through tyrants, heretics, and false brethren, and instigating the whole world against them.

The right, practical divinity is this: Believe in Christ, and do thy duty in that state of life to which God has called thee.

I fear the axe is laid to the root of the tree, soon to cut it down. God of His infinite mercy take us graciously away, that we may not be present at such calamities.

The faith toward God in Christ must be sure and steadfast, that it may solace and make glad the conscience, and put it to rest. When a man has this certainty, he has overcome the serpent.

But faith is a thing in the heart, having its being and substance by itself, given of God as His proper work, not a corporal thing, that may be seen, felt, or touched.

No greater mischief can happen to a Christian people, than to have God's Word taken from them, or falsified, so that they no longer have it pure and clear.

We take pains to conciliate the good will and friendship of men, that so they may show us a favorable countenance; how much the more ought we to conciliate our Lord Jesus, that so He may be gracious unto us.

I hate myself, that I cannot believe it so constantly and surely as I should; but no human creature can rightly know how mercifully God is inclined toward those that steadfastly believe in Christ.

In all things, in the least creatures, and their members, God's almighty power and wonderful works clearly shine. For what man, how powerful, wise, and holy soever, can make out of one fig, a fig tree?

Now, to give grace, peace, everlasting life, forgiveness of sins, to justify, to save, to deliver from death and hell, surely these are not the works of any creature, but of the sole majesty of God, things which the angels themselves can neither create nor give.

All the works of God are unsearchable and unspeakable, no human sense can find them out.

Truly, if God were to give an account to every one of his works and actions, He were but a poor, simple God.

When God contemplates some great work, He begins it by the hand of some poor, weak, human creature, to whom He afterwards gives aid.

Where human help is at an end, God's help begins.

He that has not God, let him have else what he will, is more miserable than Lazarus, who lay at the rich man's gate, and was starved to death.

The resurrection of our Savior Christ, in the preaching of the gospel, raises earthquakes in the world now, as when Christ arose out of the sepulchre bodily.

Ah, how impious and ungrateful is the world, thus to condemn and persecute God's ineffable grace!

I hold that the name Paradise applies to the whole world.

When one asked, where God was before heaven was created? St Augustine answered: He was in Himself. When another asked me the same question, I said: He was building hell for such idle, presumptuous, fluttering and inquisitive spirits as you.

Our blessed Savior Christ himself preaches that the Holy Ghost is everlasting and Almighty God.

For we must first hear the Word, and then afterwards the Holy Ghost works in our hearts; He works in the hearts of whom He will, and how He will, but never without the Word.

He that can humble himself earnestly before God in Christ, has already won.

We easily fall into idolatry, for we are inclined thereunto by nature, and coming to us by inheritance, it seems pleasant.

Whoso hearkens not to God's voice, is an idolater, though he performs the highest and most heavy service of God.

Christ, our high priest, is ascended into heaven, and sits on the right hand of God the Father, where, without ceasing, He makes intercession for us.

Without Christ, God will not be found, known, or comprehended.

The words of our Savior Christ are exceeding powerful; they have hands and feet; they outdo the utmost subtleties of the worldly wise.

The mystery of the humanity of Christ, that He sunk himself into our flesh, is beyond all human understanding.

For the law rules and governs mankind; therefore the law judges mankind, and not mankind the law.

The god of the world is riches, pleasure, and pride, wherewith it abuses all the creatures and gifts of God.

If a man serves not God only, then surely he serves the devil.

He must be of a high and great spirit that undertakes to serve the people in body and soul, for he must suffer the utmost danger and unthankfulness.

When a man will serve God, he must not look upon that which he does; not upon the work, but how it ought to be done, and whether God has commanded it or no.

Christ brings also peace, but not as the apostles brought it, through preaching; He gives it as a Creator, as His own proper creature.

To comfort a sorrowful conscience is much better than to possess many kingdoms; yet the world regards it not; nay, condemns it, calling us rebels, disturbers of the peace.

But this holy function of preaching the Word is, by Satan, fiercely resisted; he would willingly have it utterly suppressed, for thereby his kingdom is destroyed.

God will have His servants to be repenting sinners, standing in fear of His anger, of the devil, death, and hell, and believing in Christ.

God only, and not wealth, maintains the world; riches merely make people proud and lazy.

For my part, I am a poor sinner, and that I am sure of out of God's Word.

Heaven and earth, all the emperors, kings, and princes of the world, could not raise a fit dwelling-place for God; yet, in a weak human soul, that keeps His Word, He willingly resides.

In the meantime, though misfortune, misery, and trouble be upon us, we must have this sure confidence in Him, that He will not suffer us to be destroyed either in body or soul, but will so deal with us, that all things, be they good or evil, shall redound to our advantage.

When I consider my crosses, tribulations, and temptations, I shame myself almost to death, thinking what are they in comparison of the sufferings of my blessed Savior Christ Jesus.

God delights in our temptations, and yet hates them; He delights in them when they drive us to prayer; He hates them when they drive us to despair.

God has His measuring lines and His canons, called the Ten Commandments; they are written in our flesh and blood: the sum of them is this: "What thou wouldest have done to thyself, the same do thou to another."

The highest and most precious treasure we receive of God is, that we can speak, hear, see, etc.; but how few acknowledge these as God's special gifts, much less give God thanks for them.

The most acceptable service we can do and show unto God, and which alone He desires of us, is, that He be praised of us.

Oh! His grace and goodness towards us is so immeasurably great, that without great assaults and trials it cannot be understood.

Superstition, idolatry, and hypocrisy have ample wages, but truth goes a begging.

The great men and the doctors understand not the word of God, but it is revealed to the humble and to children.

Wealth is the smallest thing on earth, the least gift that God has bestowed on mankind. What is it in comparison with God's Word?

When we have our sweet and loving Savior Christ, we are rich and happy more than enough; we care nothing for their state, honor, and wealth.

Should we then admire our own wisdom? I, for my part, admit myself a fool, and yield myself captive.

All the wisdom of the world is childish foolishness in comparison with the acknowledgment of Christ.

I have lived to see the greatest plague on earth—the condemning of God's Word, a fearful thing, surpassing all other plagues in the world.

If I were addicted to God's Word at all times alike, and always had such love and desire thereunto as sometimes I have, then should I account myself the most blessed man on earth.

Once sure that the doctrine we teach is God's Word, once certain of this, we may build thereupon, and know that this cause shall and must remain; the devil shall not be able to overthrow it, much less the world be able to uproot it, how fiercely soever it rage.

I have before me God's Word which cannot fail, nor can the gates of hell prevail against it; thereby will I remain, though the whole world be against me.

A man's word is a little sound, that flies into the air, and soon vanishes; but the Word of God is greater than heaven and earth.

The Word is sure, and fails not, though heaven and earth must pass away.

For God's Word is a light that shines in a dark place, as all examples of faith show.

We are but the instruments or assistants, by whom God works.

The world seems to me like a decayed house, David and the prophets being the spars, and Christ the main pillar in the midst, that supports all.

He who loses sight of the Word of God, falls into despair; the voice of heaven no longer sustains him; he follows only the disorderly tendency of his heart, and of world vanity, which lead him on to his destruction.

We must not regard what or how the world esteems us, so we have the Word pure, and are certain of our doctrine.

Martin Luther's Table Talk (c. 1546)

If I am not convinced by proof from holy scripture, or by cogent reasons, if I am not satisfied by the very text I have cited, and if my judgment is not in this way brought into subjection to God's Word, I neither can nor will retract anything.

Address to the Diet of Worms (1521)

For gluttony, drunkenness, lying late abed, loafing and being without work are weapons of unchastity, with which chastity is quickly overcome.

For they who think they make an end of temptation by yielding to it, only set themselves on fire the more.

The strongest defense is prayer and the Word of God; namely, that when evil lust stirs, a man flee to prayer, call upon God's mercy and help, read and meditate on the Gospel, and in it consider Christ's sufferings.

Neither silver, gold, precious stones, nor any rare thing has such manifold alloys and flaws as have good works, which ought to have a single simple goodness, and without it are mere color, show, and deceit.

Although we cannot all be writers, we all want to be critics.

We ought first to know that there are no good works except those which God has commanded, even as there is no sin except that which God has forbidden.

The first and highest, the most precious of all good works is faith in Christ.

If men want to praise us and not God in us, we are not to endure it, but with all our powers forbid it and flee from it as from the most grievous sin and robbery of divine honor.

Yet we must not despair if we are not soon rid of the temptation, nor by any means imagine that we are free from it as long as we live, and we must regard it only as an incentive and admonition to prayer, fasting, watching, laboring.

A Treatise on Good Works (1520)

LUTZER, ERWIN

Born in Regina, Saskatchewan, in 1941, Erwin Lutzer has been the pastor of Moody Church in Chicago since 1980. Under his leadership the church has grown significantly, adding a Christian Life Center to the original building.

He is the regular speaker on three radio programs: *Songs in the Night*, *Running to Win*, and *The Moody Church Hour*. His church sermons are broadcast live across the Internet every Sunday.

His written works include *One Minute after You Die: A Preview of Your Final Destination*; *The Da Vinci Deception*; *Hitler's Cross*; *Oprah, Miracles, and the New Earth: A Critique*; and *The Truth about Same-Sex Marriage: 6 Things You Need to Know about What's Really at Stake*.

It has been correctly said that the ground is level at the foot of the cross. We all come as needy sinners; we all come with the same need for the pardon that God alone can give us.

Anyone who takes the Bible seriously knows that it is often intolerant and discriminatory. It is intolerant of sexual sins among heterosexuals and homosexuals; it loudly discriminates against those who do a variety of evils and those who believe false doctrine. It especially discriminates against those who refuse to accept Jesus as Savior and teaches that they shall be in hell forever.

The Truth about Same-Sex Marriage (2004)

When you come to Christ, you do not come to give, you come to receive. You do not come to try your best, you come to trust. You do not come just to be helped, but to be rescued. You do not come to be made better (although that does happen), you come to be made alive!

If God is satisfied with the death of Christ, we should be too.

How You Can Be Sure That You Will Spend Eternity with God (1996)

Confession means that we agree with God. We agree that we have sinned. We agree that we are responsible for our sins. And we agree that God has the right to rid us of this sin.

When we have done something wrong, we must suppress our natural instinct to run and hide and instead come into God's presence as we are, without excuses or pretense.

After You've Blown It (2004)

Only those who see themselves as utterly destitute can fully appreciate the grace of God.

Often we assume that God is unable to work in spite of our weaknesses, mistakes, and sins. We forget that God is a specialist; He is well able to work our failures into His plans.

Failure: The Back Door to Success (1975)

MACARTHUR, JOHN

John Fullerton MacArthur Jr., who was born in Los Angeles in 1939, is the author of *The MacArthur Study Bible*, which has sold more than a million copies. He has been pastor and teacher at Grace Community Church in Sun Valley, California, since 1969. He also serves as president of The Master's College in Newhall and The Master's Seminary in Sun Valley.

Considered a fundamentalist with leanings toward Calvinism, John MacArthur has often represented the evangelical Christian community in the popular media. *Christianity Today* cites him as one of the most influential preachers of his lifetime.

His written works include *The MacArthur Study Bible, Our Sufficiency in Christ, Think Biblically: Recovering a Christian Worldview,* and *Twelve Extraordinary Women: How God Shaped Women of the Bible and What He Wants to Do with You.*

✍

The Bible is God's inspired Word—not a mere collection of various writers' opinions, ideas, philosophies, or "inspired" thoughts.

If the Bible is perfect and without error, it follows logically that we must present it as the most authoritative book in the world—the one document that contains the last word on truth.

Nothing but the Truth (1999)

Certainly God can bless America, but the necessary prelude to national blessing is a sweeping spiritual renewal that begins with individual repentance and faith in the Lord Jesus Christ. Apart from such a profound spiritual awakening and a decisive return to the God of scripture, we have no right as a nation to anticipate anything but God's judgment.

If God is going to bless America, it will not be for the sake of the nation itself. He blesses the nation, and has always done so, for the sake of His people. If we who are called by His name are not fulfilling the conditions for divine blessing, there is no hope whatsoever for the rest of the nation.

Can God Bless America? (2002)

It is important for every Christian to keep in mind the great difference between his position and his practice, his standing and his state. God sees us as righteous, because He sees us through His righteous Son, who has taken our place, and because He has planted in us a righteous new nature.

When we are willing to open our mouths to speak for Him, we can be sure that He will give us the right thing to say. It is not that we put our minds in neutral but that we submit our minds to Him to use as He sees fit and to empower as He has promised.

1 Corinthians (1984)

We step out of bounds when we conclude that anything God does isn't fair.

The urgency of the gospel is utterly lost when the preacher denies the reality or severity of everlasting punishment.

Ashamed of the Gospel (1993)

The Bible gives a clear and cogent account of the beginnings of the cosmos and humanity. There is absolutely no reason for an intelligent mind to balk at accepting it as a literal account of the origin of our universe. Although the biblical account clashes at many points with naturalistic and evolutionary hypotheses, it is not in conflict with a single scientific fact.

The evolutionary lie is so pointedly antithetical to Christian truth that it would seem unthinkable for evangelical Christians to compromise with evolutionary science in any degree.

The Battle for the Beginning (2001)

Master the truth to refute error.

When warm and fuzzy moral messages, peppered with cute anecdotes and an occasional skit, replace the meat of God's Word, the consequences are devastating.

Fool's Gold? (2005)

God is the consummate forgiver. And we depend every day on His ongoing forgiveness for our sins. The least we can do is emulate His forgiveness in our dealings with one another.

Forgiveness. Nothing is more foreign to sinful human nature. And nothing is more characteristic of divine grace.

The Freedom and Power of Forgiveness (1998)

The picture of divine sovereignty in scripture is that God positively ordains whatsoever comes to pass. He always acts with a purpose. Even the wicked unwittingly do his bidding, and thus they fulfill His sovereign purpose in the end.

Truth is that which is consistent with the mind, will, character, glory, and being of God. Even more to the point: truth is the self-expression of God.

The Truth War (2007)

As children of God we have a single goal—treasure in heaven; a single vision—God's purposes; and a single Master—God, not money.

The real challenge of Christian living is not to eliminate every uncomfortable circumstance from our lives, but to trust our sovereign, wise, good, and powerful God in the midst of every situation. Things that might trouble us such as the way we look, the way others treat us, or where we live or work can actually be sources of strength, not weakness.

Anxiety Attacked (1993)

Our fellowship with God is not meant to wait until we are in heaven. God's greatest desire, and our greatest need, is to be in constant fellowship with Him now, and there is no greater expression or experience of fellowship than prayer.

The essence of prayer is simply talking to God as you would to a beloved friend—without pretense or flippancy.

Alone with God (1995)

Let your theology rise above your circumstances.

Grace to You (2009)

The most beautiful kind of woman is the woman with a meek, gentle, peaceful, calm, quiet disposition.

The lovely, gracious, gentle submission of a Christian woman to her unsaved husband is the strongest evangelistic tool she has. It is not what she says, it is what she is.

How to Win Your Unsaved Spouse (1990)

MacDonald, George

George MacDonald, born in 1824, was a Scottish minister who came to fame through his novels and poetry. His stories, with their barely disguised messages of faith and spirituality, impressed many contemporaries. Mark Twain came to call him a friend, and C. S. Lewis called him a master. G. K. Chesterton insisted MacDonald's writing changed his very existence.

His Universalist views often caused problems with the churches where he preached. He was editor of *Good Words for the Young* and toured the States on the lecture circuit from 1872 to 1873.

His use of fantasy to convey a message of faith also influenced J. R. R. Tolkien, the author of the Lord of the Rings series. He lived until 1905, passing away in Ashtead, England.

His books include *Phantastes, At the Back of the North Wind, The Day Boy and the Night Girl, Sir Gibbie,* and *The Princess and the Goblin.*

☞

But if obedience, Lord, in me do grow
I shall one day be better than I know.

Lord, Thou hast called me forth, I turn and call on Thee.

We make, but Thou art the creating core.

My prayers, my God, flow from what I am not; I think Thy answers make me
what I am.

Help me to walk by the other light supreme,
Which shows Thy facts behind man's vaguely hinting dream.

Look deep, yet deeper, in my heart, and there,
Beyond where I can feel, read Thou the prayer.

Where I am most perplexed, it may be there
Thou mak'st a secret chamber, holy-dim,
Where Thou wilt come to help my deepest prayer.

My Lord, I find that nothing else will do,
But follow where Thou goest, sit at Thy feet,
And where I have Thee not, still run to meet.

Faith opens all the windows to God's wind.

Afresh I seek Thee. Lead me—once more I pray—
Even should it be against my will, Thy way.

Let me no more from out Thy presence go,
But keep me waiting watchful for Thy will—
Even while I do it, waiting watchful still.

I am a beast until I love as God doth love.

Diary of an Old Soul (1880)

But it is not obedience alone that our Lord will have, but obedience to the
truth, that is, to the Light of the World, truth beheld and known.

Nothing is required of man that is not first in God. It is because God is perfect that we are required to be perfect.

Whosoever gives a cup of cold water to a little one refreshes the heart of the
Father.

What is the kingdom of Christ? A rule of love, of truth—a rule of service. The
king is the chief servant in it.

Is it like the Son of man to pick out the beautiful child, and leave the common child unnoticed?

"The Child in the Midst" sermon (19th century)

Christ is God's Forgiveness.

To men who are not simple, simple words are the most inexplicable of riddles.

If it be the truth, we shall one day see it another thing than it appears now, and love it because we see it lovely; for all truth is lovely.

A man will say: "I forgive, but I cannot forget. Let the fellow never come in my sight again." To what does such a forgiveness reach? To the remission or sending away of the penalties which the wronged believes he can claim from the wrongdoer. But there is no sending away of the wrong itself from between them.

"It Shall Not Be Forgiven" sermon (19th century)

Do you count it a great faith to believe what God has said? It seems to me, I repeat, a little faith, and, if alone, worthy of reproach. To believe what He has not said is faith indeed, and blessed. For that comes of believing in Him.

Our God, we will trust Thee. Shall we not find Thee equal to our faith? One day, we shall laugh ourselves to scorn that we looked for so little from Thee; for Thy giving will not be limited by our hoping.

Ah Lord! be Thou in all our being; as not in the Sundays of our time alone.

They are blessed to whom a wonder is not a fable, to whom a mystery is not a mockery, to whom a glory is not an unreality—who are content to ask, "Is it like Him?"

"The Higher Faith" sermon (19th century)

Nothing is inexorable but love.

Love is one, and love is changeless. For love loves unto purity.

As it was love that first created humanity, so even human love, in proportion to its divinity, will go on creating the beautiful for its own outpouring.

To see a truth, to know what it is, to understand it, and to love it, are all one.

It is the nature of God, so terribly pure that it destroys all that is not pure as fire, which demands like purity in our worship. He will have purity. It is not that the fire will burn us if we do not worship thus; but that the fire will burn us until we worship thus.

"The Consuming Fire" sermon (19th century)

A man must not choose his neighbor; he must take the neighbor that God sends him. In him, whoever he be, lies, hidden or revealed, a beautiful brother.

"Love Thy Neighbor" sermon (19th century)

MACHEN, J. GRESHAM

John Gresham Machen was a professor of the New Testament at Princeton Theological Seminary. In response to "modernist" interpretations and influences, he founded the Westminster Theological Seminary to promote a more orthodox understanding of faith.

He and a group of conservative friends left the Presbyterian Church in protest over what was seen as liberal teaching and formed the Orthodox Presbyterian Church. He taught New Testament studies at Westminster for the rest of his life. His teachings and the institutions he helped found are still influential today.

Born in 1881 in Baltimore, Maryland, he died in 1937 in Bismarck, North Dakota.

His written works include *Christianity and Liberalism, New Testament Greek for Beginners, What Is Faith?,* and *The New Testament: An Introduction to Its Literature and History.*

If all creeds are equally true, then since they are contradictory to one another, they are all equally false, or at least equally uncertain.

Indifferentism about doctrine makes no heroes of the faith.

The doctrine of God and the doctrine of man are the two great presuppositions of the gospel.

According to Christian belief, man exists for the sake of God; according to the liberal church, in practice if not in theory, God exists for the sake of man.

The Sermon on the Mount, like all the rest of the New Testament, really leads a man straight to the foot of the cross.

Light may seem at times to be an impertinent intruder, but it is always beneficial in the end.

It never occurred to Paul that a gospel might be true for one man and not for another; the blight of pragmatism had never fallen upon his soul.

The truth is, the God of modern preaching, though He may perhaps be very good, is rather uninteresting.

The type of religion which rejoices in the pious sound of traditional phrases, regardless of their meanings, or shrinks from "controversial" matters, will never stand amid the shocks of life.

The truth is that when men speak of trust in Jesus' Person as being possible without acceptance of the message of His death and resurrection, they do not really mean trust at all.

Christianity and Liberalism (1923)

The Cross was a shameful thing; the proclamation of a crucified Messiah appeared, therefore, to the devout Pharisee as an outrageous blasphemy.

The religion of Paul was rooted altogether in the redeeming work of Jesus Christ. Jesus for Paul was primarily not a Revealer, but a Savior.

Those who speak of the transformation wrought in Paul by the appearance of Jesus as magical or mechanical or inconceivable have never reflected upon the mysteries of personal intercourse.

The Origin of Paul's Religion (1921)

MANNING, BRENNAN

Born in New York City in 1934, Richard Francis Xavier Manning (known as Brennan) was a marine during the Korean War, serving as a sportswriter for the Marine Corps newspaper. After the war he trained to be a Franciscan monk. His new lifestyle involved working as a water-carrier and dishwasher, and becoming a hermit. He was a liturgy instructor and spiritual director at St. Francis Seminary, where he and other monks worked as shrimpers, hoping to influence those "unchurched" working in the industry.

After a battle with alcoholism he began writing in earnest. The success of his books led to his being in great demand as a speaker. His message was one of God's unconditional love through Jesus.

He died in 2013, in Belmar, New Jersey.

His books include *The Ragamuffin Gospel*, *Abba's Child*, and the memoir *All Is Grace*.

Contemplative awareness of the risen Jesus shapes our resemblance to Him and turns us into the persons God intended us to be.

Define yourself radically as one beloved by God. This is the true self. Every other identity is illusion.

Abba's Child: The Cry of the Heart for Intimate Belonging (1994)

It breaks God's heart that we run from instead of to Him when we fail.

We have spread so many coats of whitewash over the historical Jesus that we scarcely see the glow of His presence anymore.

Posers, Fakers, and Wannabes (2003)

My deepest awareness of myself is that I am deeply loved by Jesus Christ and I have done nothing to earn it or deserve it.

The temptation of the age is to look good without being good.

The Ragamuffin Gospel: Good News for the Bedraggled,
Beat-Up, and Burnt Out (2000)

..., when I feel that what I'm doing is insignificant and unimportant, help ...e to remember that everything I do is significant and important in Your eyes, because You love me and You put me here, and no one else can do what I am doing in exactly the way I do it.

Souvenirs of Solitude: Finding Rest in Abba's Embrace (2009)

Real freedom is freedom from the opinions of others. Above all, freedom from your opinions about yourself.

The Wisdom of Tenderness: What Happens When God's Fierce Mercy Transforms Our Lives (2004)

The gospel is absurd and the life of Jesus is meaningless unless we believe that He lived, died, and rose again with but one purpose in mind: to make a brand-new creation. Not to make people with better morals but to create a community of prophets and professional lovers, men and women who would surrender to the mystery of the fire of the Spirit that burns within, who would live in ever greater fidelity to the omnipresent Word of God, who would enter into the center of it all, the very heart and mystery of Christ, into the center of the flame that consumes, purifies, and sets everything aglow with peace, joy, boldness, and extravagant, furious love. This, my friend, is what it really means to be a Christian.

The Furious Longing of God (2009)

MARSHALL, CATHERINE

Catherine Marshall, born in Johnson City, Tennessee, in 1914, was the daughter, mother, and wife of Presbyterian ministers and a successful author in her own right. Her husband, Peter Marshall, was twice appointed chaplain to the US Senate.

Two years after her husband's death in 1949, she wrote his biography, titled *A Man Called Peter*. Another family member, her mother, was the inspiration for her book *Christy*. Both books were later adapted for film and television.

Her second husband, Leonard LeSourd, was the editor of *Guideposts* magazine for twenty-eight years. Together they founded the Chosen Books company.

Catherine died in 1983 in Washington, DC.

Her books include compilations of Peter Marshall's sermons and prayers, *A Man Called Peter*, *Christy*, *Catherine Marshall's Story Bible*, *My Personal Prayer Diary*, *The Helper*, and *To Live Again*.

Satan cannot create anything new, cannot create anything at all. He must steal what God has created. Thus he twists love and God's wonderful gift of sex into lust and sadism and myriad perversions. He disfigures the heart's deep desire to worship God and persuades us to bow before lesser gods of lust or money or power.

Despite disappointments, the Christian is obligated to pray for the sick because we are bidden to do so and because the crumb of our caring is but a morsel broken from the whole loaf of the Father's infinite and tender love.

Something More (1974)

The cross stands as the final symbol that no evil exists that God cannot turn into a blessing. He is the living Alchemist who can take the dregs from the slag-heaps of life—disappointment, frustration, sorrow, disease, death, economic loss, heartache—and transform the dregs into gold.

No man is worthy to rule until he has been ruled; no man can lead well until he has given himself to leadership greater than his own.

Beyond Ourselves (1961)

Evil is real—and powerful. It has to be fought, not explained away, not fled. And God is against evil all the way. So each of us has to decide where *we* stand, how we're going to live *our* lives. We can try to persuade ourselves that evil doesn't exist; live for ourselves and wink at evil. We can say that it isn't so bad after all, maybe even try to call it fun by clothing it in silks and velvets. We can compromise with it, keep quiet about it, and say it's none of our business. Or we can work on God's side, listen for His orders on strategy against the evil, no matter how horrible it is, and know that He can transform it.

A Christian has no business being satisfied with mediocrity. He's supposed to reach for the stars. Why not? He's not on his own anymore. He has God's help now.

Christy (1967)

McDowell, Josh

Born in Union City, Michigan, in 1939, Josh McDowell came from a family background of alcoholism and abuse. While serving in the Air National Guard, he sustained a head injury that led to his discharge.

Later while studying law, he decided to write a paper disproving the existence of Christ through historical evidence, but that endeavor had the opposite effect: he eventually obtained his master of divinity degree from Talbot Theological Seminary.

His paper "disproving" Christianity became the book *Evidence That Demands a Verdict*, and his speaking ministry often addresses the questions of nonbelievers. His childhood experiences led to his also addressing matters of sexuality and self-esteem.

He is a founder of Josh.org and Operation Carelift, a humanitarian aid organization.

His books include *Evidence That Demands a Verdict*, *His Image My Image*, *How to Help Your Child Say "No" to Sexual Pressure*, and *Evidence for the Historical Jesus*.

✍🏻

Our purpose in life is to know God and become more and more like Him.

The Bible is the means God has chosen to reach out in human language, reveal the essence of His rational heart, and relate the Good News of His redemptive plan.

Beyond Belief to Conviction (with Bob Hostetler, 2002)

Christ did not come to earth to teach Christianity—Christ is Christianity.

It is no coincidence that the fear of God largely disappeared from our culture at about the same time that relativism and subjective believing became prevalent.

The Last Christian Generation (2006)

My heart and mind were created to work in harmony together. Never has an individual been called upon to commit intellectual suicide in trusting Christ as Savior and Lord.

You can laugh at Christianity; you can mock and ridicule it. But it works. It changes lives. If you trust Christ, start watching your attitudes and actions, because Jesus Christ is in the business of changing lives.

More Than a Carpenter (1977)

Fatherhood may be the most frightening job in the world but it is also the most important and most rewarding job a man can tackle.

Fathering is indeed a privilege given by the Lord—a matchless opportunity to pour our lives into those we love so dearly.

The Father Connection (1996)

Obedience to God's commands not only protects us from harm; it also allows God to provide for us, sometimes in breathtaking ways.

Truth is objective because God exists outside ourselves; it is universal because God is above all; it is constant because God is eternal. Absolute truth is absolute because it originates from the original.

Right from Wrong (with Bob Hostetler, 1994)

Christ can be trusted to keep His Word that He will exchange our drab existence for joyous living, abundant life! And while true love, total acceptance, and complete security are rare in our frantic world, the biblical evidence that our desires in these areas will be fulfilled in Christ is abundant.

Evidence about God provides a basis for faith that meets your needs for being loved, accepted, and secure; and that kind of faith yields joy.

Evidence for Joy (1984)

There are many claims that various gods exist, but only one God cared enough to become a man and die on our behalf.

Because God is holy, He cannot look on sin with indifference.

Evidence for the Resurrection (with Sean MacDowell, 2009)

MEYER, F. B.

Frederick Brotherton Meyer, who was born in London in 1847, was a proponent of the Higher Life approach in England in the late nineteenth century. This movement promoted the idea of a second experience of grace enabling the recipient to move from his or her original state to a holier, more Christlike state.

He was also a friend of evangelist D. L. Moody. While Moody was touring England, Meyer hosted him and provided him with introductions. Moody later returned the favor when Meyer toured the States. The two became lifelong friends, and Meyer later wrote a biography of Moody.

Meyer was an evangelical Baptist minister who concentrated on social reform and inner-city missions. The British newspaper the *Daily Telegraph* dubbed him "the Archbishop of the Free Churches." He died in 1929.

His written works include *The Prophet of Hope*, *Saved and Kept*, *Christ in Isaiah*, and *Trial by Fire*.

✍

For every one that definitely turns his back on Christ, there are hundreds who drift from Him. Life's ocean is full of currents, any one of which will sweep us past the harbor-mouth even when we seem nearest to it, and carry us far out to sea.

Thy best Friend is the Lord of Providence. Thy Brother is Prime Minister of the universe, and holds the keys of the divine commissariat.

Our sins are so deep-dyed, so inveterate, so fast, that nothing but blood could set us free. Blood must atone for us. Blood must cleanse us.

We need not deny that other men have been illuminated; but the difference between illumination and inspiration is as far as the east is from the west.

We should read the Bible as those who listen to the very speech of God.

The world is full of religious books; but the man who has fed his religious life upon the Bible will tell in a moment the difference between them and the scriptures of the Old and New Testaments.

He is the prop which underpins creation. Christ, and not fate. Christ, and not nature.

Creation is the vesture of Christ. He wraps himself about in its ample folds.

The Way into the Holiest (1893)

It is the business of the shepherd to lead the willing sheep aright.

It is our part to allow as small a space as possible to intervene between His footsteps and our own.

Faith puts Christ between itself and circumstances so that it cannot see them.

Would that we had the faith to look upon every trying circumstance, from every fretting worry, from every annoyance and temptation, into the face of our Guide, and say, "It is the right way, Thou great Shepherd of the sheep; lead Thou me on!"

We must be willing to be led.

Do not judge God's ways while they are in progress. Wait till the plan is complete.

Christ's leadings are always along "paths of righteousness."

Your salvation does not depend on what you are but on what He is. For every look at self, take ten looks at Christ.

Unbelief puts circumstances between itself and Christ, so as to not see Him.

The Shepherd Psalm (1889)

You do not test the resources of God till you try the impossible.

The Missionary Review of the World (1913)

MEYER, JOYCE

Born in St. Louis, Missouri, in 1943, Joyce Meyer describes herself as someone who had no knowledge, didn't go to church, and had a bundle of problems. But she prayed to God one day while driving to work and heard Him call her name. She joined a charismatic church and eventually founded her own ministry (initially called Life in the Word) and began broadcasting on radio and television.

A large part of her success seems to be due to her ability to talk about personal experiences such as abuse, adultery, and divorce, showing how God can lead people through these experiences to the higher lands beyond.

She was recently rated seventeenth in *Time* magazine's list of the twenty-five most influential evangelicals in America.

Her books include *Beauty for Ashes*, *The Everyday Life Bible*, and *Change Your Words, Change Your Life*.

✍

God wants us to be ourselves so that we can fulfill the call He has placed on our lives.

Without the reverential fear and awe of God, we quickly become people pleasers instead of God pleasers.

Do It Afraid! (1996)

You have to learn to be happy when other people get what you're still waiting for.

Sometimes when you are going forward spiritually, you go backwards in the natural because when our natural circumstances don't suit us, that's when we press in spiritually with God.

"Overcoming Fear with Faith" sermon (2009)

The fear of failure is crippling because it holds people back from acting on their desires, and it will certainly hinder you from fulfilling your destiny.

God wants you to be an "eagle Christian," one who can fly high, be bold, live with power, keep circumstances and relationships in perspective, live at peace, stay strong, and soar above the storms of life.

Never Give Up! (2008)

God has an individual plan for each person. If you will go to Him and submit to Him, He will come into your heart and commune with you. He will teach and guide you in the way you should go.

The Lord wants to be personally involved in our lives. He wants to be involved with us in the grocery store checkout line. He wants to be involved with us when we get caught in a traffic jam and can't move.

If Not for the Grace of God (1995)

I want you to be encouraged that in God's time you will see the dreams and visions that God has given you fulfilled.

Learn to enjoy waiting, realizing that waiting is what will deliver your dream.

When, God, When? (1994)

There is no danger of developing eyestrain from looking on the bright side of things, so why not try it?

Get up every day, love God, and do your best.

Approval Addiction (2005)

Courage is fear that has said its prayers and decided to go forward anyway.

I Dare You: Embrace Life with Passion (2009)

I may not be where I need to be but I thank God I am not where I used to be.

Woman to Woman: Candid Conversations from Me to You (2007)

One mistake does not have to rule a person's entire life.

It is impossible to be both selfish and happy.

Any Minute (with Deborah Bradford, 2009)

Our past may explain why we're suffering but we must not use it as an excuse to stay in bondage.

You cannot have a positive life and a negative mind.

Battlefield of the Mind: Winning the Battle in Your Mind (2009)

God wants you to be delivered from what you have done and from what has been done to you. Both are equally important to Him.

Beauty for Ashes: Receiving Emotional Healing (2003)

MOODY, D. L.

Born in Northfield, Massachusetts, in 1837, Dwight Lyman Moody had a difficult start in life. Along with his siblings he often had to work for food. His Sunday school teacher later reported that he had seldom seen a child so spiritually dark and doubted that God would get much good out of him.

But Moody proved him wrong. He surrendered his life to God and went on to start a church in an abandoned building. The congregation grew so large so quickly that President Lincoln paid it a visit.

In 1871 he met gospel singer Ira Sankey, and the two began a now legendary series of evangelical tours of Britain and the United States. People turned out in the thousands to hear them.

He founded the Moody Church, Northfield School, Mount Hermon School, the Moody Bible Institute, and Moody Publishers.

He died in 1899 in the same town in which he was born.

His written works include *Heaven*, *Secret Power*, and *The Ten Commandments*.

☛

The moral man is as guilty as the rest. His morality cannot save him.

Let your confession be as wide as your transgression.

Lust is the devil's counterfeit for love. There is nothing more beautiful on earth than a pure love and there is nothing so blighting as lust.

If you don't enter the kingdom of heaven by God's way, you cannot enter at all.

It is a favorite thing with infidels to set their own standard, to measure themselves by other people. But that will not do in the Day of Judgment. Now we will use God's law as a balance weight.

Satan is willing to have us worship anything, however sacred—the Bible, the crucifix, the church—if only we do not worship God Himself.

God will not accept a divided heart. He must be absolute monarch.

We have got nowadays so that we divide lies into white lies and black lies, society lies and business lies, etc. The Word of God knows no such letting-down of the standard.

I believe the memory is "the worm that never dies". . .the memory is never cleansed of obscene stories and unclean acts. Even if a man repents and reforms he often has to fight the past.

What will your university education amount to, and all your wealth and honors if you go down through lust and passion and covetousness, and lose your soul at last?

Weighed and Wanting (c. 1896)

I have no sympathy with the idea that God puts us behind the blood and saves us, and then leaves us in Egypt to be under the old taskmaster. I believe God brings us out of Egypt into the promised land, and that it is the privilege of every child of God to be delivered from every foe, from every besetting sin.

We are all the time coming to the end of things here—the end of the week, the end of the month, the end of the year, the end of school days. It is end, end, end all the time. But, thank God, He is going to satisfy us with long life; no end to it, an endless life.

I hunted all through the four Gospels trying to find one of Christ's funeral sermons, but I couldn't find any. I found He broke up every funeral He ever attended! Death couldn't exist where He was.

"The Ninety-First Psalm" sermon (late 19th century)

Man lost life by unbelief—by not believing God's word; and we get life back again by believing—by taking God at His word.

Heaven is filled with a company of those who have been *twice born*.

The Bible teaches us that man by nature is lost and guilty, and our experience confirms this.

When Christ cried out on Calvary, "It is finished!" He meant what He said. All that men have to do now is just accept the work of Jesus Christ.

The Way to God (1884)

If there is a cry coming up from a heart broken on account of sin, God will hear that cry.

The longest time man has to live has no more proportion to eternity than a drop of dew has to the ocean.

The society of heaven will be select. No one who studies scripture can doubt that.

No one that is not of a contrite and humble spirit will dwell with God in His high and holy place.

There are a good many kinds of aristocracy in this world, but the aristocracy of heaven will be holiness.

Heaven (1881)

You will never have true pleasure or peace or joy or comfort until you have found Christ.

"Excuses" sermon (1880)

I have heard of a great many people who think if they are united to the church, and have made one profession, that will do for all the rest of their days. But there is a cross for every one of us daily.

"Where Art Thou?" sermon (1880)

Our failure is that preachers ignore the Cross, and veil Christ with sapless sermons and superfine language.

The world can get on very well without you and me, but the world cannot get on without Christ, and therefore we must testify of Him.

Let us seek to be useful. Let us seek to be vessels fit for the Master's use, that God, the Holy Spirit, may shine fully through us.

We have to take the Word of God just as it is; and if we are going to take it, we have no authority to take out just what we like, what we think is appropriate, and let dark reason be our guide.

Let it be God's glory and not our own that we seek, and when we get to that point, how speedily the Lord will bless us for good.

Secret Power (1881)

It sometimes happens that a man, in giving to the world the truths that have most influenced his life, unconsciously writes the truest kind of a character sketch.

A Life for a Life and Other Addresses (1897)

Though sickness, or trouble, or even death itself, should come to our house, and claim our dearest ones, still they are not lost, but only gone before.

Confession follows conviction.

None will walk the celestial pavement of heaven but those washed in the blood.

Just like the moonshine, our light is borrowed light.

Some people tell us it does not make any difference what a man believes if he is only sincere. One church is just as good as another if you are only sincere. I do not believe any greater delusion ever came out of the pit of hell than that.

If God says it, let us take our stand upon it.

It is God-dishonoring to forget that He still has power, although our armies are defeated, and all seems dark and gloomy.

Why, we should say the beggar had gone mad to be running away from the Prince of Wales with the bag of gold. Sinner, that is your condition. The Prince of Heaven wants to give you eternal life, and you are running away from Him.

No man can give a satisfactory reason for the hope that is in him if he is a stranger to the "Blood."

You might say the whole plan of salvation is in two words—Giving; Receiving. God gives; I receive.

Wondrous Love (1876)

Some people do not believe in sudden conversion. I should like them to answer me when was Zaccheus converted? He was certainly in his sins when he went up into that tree; he certainly was converted when he came down.

All you have got to do is, to prove that you are a sinner, and I will prove that you have got a Savior. And the greater the sinner, the greater need you have of a Savior.

Satan offers you what he cannot give; he is a liar, and has been from the foundation of the world.

The loss of a soul! Christ knew what it meant. That is what brought Him from the bosom of the Father; that is what brought Him from the throne; that is what brought Him to Calvary.

I heard someone in the inquiry-room telling a young person to go home and seek Christ in his closet. I would not dare to tell anyone to do that. You might be dead before you got home.

If there is a man or woman in this audience tonight who believes that he or she is lost, I have good news to tell you—Christ is come after you.

You can always tell when a man is a great way from God—he is always talking about himself, and how good he is.

There are two bidders for your soul tonight. It is for you to decide which shall have it.

I pity the man who is living on the devil's promises.

"Am I saved, or am I lost?" It must be one or the other. There is no neutrality about the matter.

Best Thoughts and Discourses of D. L. Moody (1876)

It is a solemn thing to think that Christ does not remain as an uninvited guest.

If there is anything in your life which you know to be wrong, do not sleep until you have the thing settled with God.

We should not profess one thing and do the opposite. No Christian has ever bought the friendship of the world without disloyalty to Christ.

It is a great thing for a mighty God to permit sinful men like you and me to call upon Him. When men get great we cannot get a chance to call upon them, but it is not so with our God. He commands us to call.

It is a great mistake to be looking at obstacles when we have such a God to look at.

May God help us who are parents to pray continually for our children, that God will preserve them from the corrupting influences of those amongst whom they are thrown. But it is folly to pray for our children if we follow Lot's example, and run right into the devil's camp.

There will be no peace in any soul until it is willing to obey the voice of God.

The tendency to sin gathers force with every new commission. So the battle goes on in every one of us. We must either overcome sin, or it will overcome us; we must decide.

The essence of sin is obedience to our own lusts and desires, and disobedience to God.

Short Talks (late 19th century)

He only is safe for eternity who is sheltered behind the finished work of Christ.

"There Is No Difference" sermon (1880)

There is no man living who can do the work God has for me to do. No one can do it but myself.

A man can have enthusiasm in everything else, but the moment that a little fire gets in the Church, people raise the cry, "Ah, enthusiasm—false excitement—I'm afaid of that."

The Son of God passed by the mansions and went down into a manger, that he might sympathize with the lowly.

We cannot be lukewarm; we have to be on fire with the cause of Christ.

If love does not prompt all work, all work is for naught.

I have yet to find that God ever uses a man who is all the time looking on the dark side, and talking about the obstacles and looking at them, and who is discouraged and cast down.

All that a man has to answer for is for the talent or talents that God has given him.

My friends, you cannot take palsied souls to a better place than the feet of Jesus.

There are many willing to preach to thousands, but are not willing to take their seat beside one soul, and lead that soul to the blessed Jesus.

The Faithful Saying (1877)

Wouldn't it be well to give some of your bouquets before a man dies, and not go and load down his coffin? He can't enjoy them then.

"Mary and Martha" sermon (late 19th century)

I do not know how near it may be to us; it may be that some of us will be ushered very soon into the presence of the King. One gaze at Him will be enough to reward us for all we have had to bear. Yes, there is peace for the past, grace for the present, and glory for the future.

Twelve Select Sermons (1884)

If I am adopted, I have become a child; God is no longer my judge, but my Father.

Old! I wish you all felt as young as I do tonight. Why, I am only sixty-two years old! If you meet me ten million years hence, then I will be young.

There never has been a day when knowledge has been sweeping over the earth as it is at the present time. . . . But this doesn't mean that righteousness is increasing. Therefore, let us be wary.

I have no sympathy with the doctrine of universal brotherhood, and universal fatherhood; I don't believe one word of it. If a man lives in the flesh and serves the flesh, he is a child of the devil. That is pretty strong language, but it is what Christ said.

"The Eighth Chapter of Romans" sermon (late 19th century)

Christ came down to save us from a terrible hell, and any man who is cast down to hell from here must go in the full blaze of the gospel, and over the mangled body of the Son of God.

"Christ Seeking Sinners" sermon (1880)

Get near to Christ, and you will never want to go back to the world. People may call you narrow, but God uses a narrow man and a narrow woman.

Jesus Christ has no peers; there is no one to be compared with Him.

If you want power with God, just get as far from the world as you can.

It seems to me that if we get one look at Christ in His love and beauty, this world and its pleasures will look very small to us.

Did you ever think what Moses would have lost if God had excused him and let Aaron, or Caleb, or Joshua, or someone else take his place?

"The Transfiguration" sermon (late 19th century)

Every true work of God has had its bitter enemies—not only outside, but also inside—just as in the days of Nehemiah.

Pentecost isn't over yet!

The best work usually meets the strongest opposition.

"Revivals" sermon (late 19th century)

I would a thousand times rather that God's will should be done than my own.

Many people would be greatly surprised if God did answer their prayers.

Some people think God does not like to be troubled with our constant coming and asking. The only way to trouble God is not to come at all.

We are to ask with a beggar's humility, to seek with a servant's carefulness, and to knock with the confidence of a friend.

If we knock, God has promised to open the door and grant our request. It may be years before the answer comes; He may keep us knocking; but He has promised that the answer will come.

What we want is to press our case right up to the throne of God.

There was a man convicted and converted in answer to prayer. So if you are anxious about the conversion of some relative, or some friend, make up your mind that you will give God no rest, day or night, till He grants your petition.

We cannot be too frequent in our requests; God will not weary of His children's prayers.

All true prayer must be offered in full submission to God.

We must have a warrant for our prayers. If we have some great desire, we must search the scriptures to find if it be right to ask it.

Prevailing Prayer: What Hinders It? (1884)

MOORE, BETH

At age eighteen, Beth Moore (who was born in Green Bay, Wisconsin, in 1957) gave herself to God. Later, as a young mom, she decided she wanted to know more about how to live as a Christian woman and began writing a series of Bible studies. Their popularity spread, and women's groups centered around these studies sprang up.

Beth and her husband, Keith, founded Living Proof Ministries, which focuses on helping women model (or remodel) their lives along biblical principles. The ministry holds conferences around the United States and in many other countries.

She broadcasts her lessons through her radio program *Living Proof with Beth Moore* and her regular TV slot *Wednesdays in the Word*.

Her books include *Get Out of That Pit*; *So Long, Insecurity, You've Been a Bad Friend to Us*; and Bible studies including *To Live Is Christ*, *Breaking Free*, *Jesus: The One and Only*, and *Loving Well*.

If there is an area where you distrust God, underneath it is a place you've been wounded and we want Him to heal it.

I don't want any of those things I fear to happen, but this I know, if they do, my God will take care of me, my God will take care of me!

Who Will You Trust? (2007)

A high regard for the things of this world always signals a lowering regard for God.

Satan never wastes a fiery dart by aiming at a spot covered by armor. The bull's eye is located dead center in our inconsistency. That's where the enemy plans to bring us down.

Daniel (2006)

When God dwells at the center of our lives, peace and contentment will belong to us just as surely as we belong to God.

Our blessings include life and health, family and friends, freedom and possessions. . .the gifts we receive from God are multiplied when we share them.

Prayers and Promises for Women (2003)

No sin, no matter how momentarily pleasurable, comforting, or habitual, is worth missing what God has for us.

I don't know a single person who truly seems to bear the mark of God's presence and power in his or her life who hasn't been asked by God to be obedient in a way that was dramatically painful.

Believing God (2004)

Let's all wise up. Some of us aren't fighting the fire; we're playing with fire. Flirting with the devil. Stop it! Stop it now before all hell literally breaks loose.

Satan knows that the only offensive weapon we have to raise against him is the sword of the Spirit, the Word of God. He can't keep it from being powerful, but if he can tempt us to think little of it, he knows it will never be powerful in us.

Voices of the Faithful (2005)

The Bible teaches that there are no lost causes. No permanent pit-dwellers except those who refuse to leave.

I beg you to see that your enemy has a tremendous investment not only in digging and camouflaging a pit in your pathway but also, should you tumble down, in convincing you to stay there after you fall in.

Get Out of That Pit (2007)

No matter what authority Satan and his subjects have temporarily been allowed in this world system, Christ can pull rank anytime He wants to.

If you have truly repented—which means you have experienced godly sorrow and a subsequent detour from the sin—bathe yourself in the river of God's forgiveness.

Jesus: 90 Days with the One and Only (2007)

I beg you if you are not married, you do not make a marital decision out of desperation. That is no way to think. You are not ready to think that through yet. Wait until you can think straight.

Desperation does not make good decisions.

Overcoming Insecurity (2006)

Sometimes truth is costly but not nearly as costly as deception.

"My child, you believe Me for so little. Don't be so safe in the things you pray. Who are you trying to keep from looking foolish? Me or you?"

Praying God's Word (2000)

There is not a single soul that jealousy looks good on. Nobody! It looks ugly on everybody, and it makes us act ugly—it makes us act out of character.

Satan is hoping that the present situation that you are in will send you over the edge.

A Beautiful Mind (2009)

It is not about never doubting, it is about coming out on the other side with twice the faith you had going into your doubt.

He brought my life passion from my life pain.

Wrestling with God (2009)

One of the things that I've said to God so many times is, never let my zeal in public exceed my zeal in private.

Don't let me get out there somewhere and get a big thing going that was not true this morning just between the two of us, Lord Jesus.

Life Today (1996)

Satan cannot get inside a believer, but sexual seduction is one of the most powerful ways the fires of hell can burn the outside of a believer. The sin is forgiven the moment the person repents, but healing from the ramifications can take longer.

God desires more than anything to restore sexual purity to those who have been sexually seduced, but it takes time to peel away the damaged character. The pain that can be involved in the process demands much trust in a good and loving God.

When Godly People Do Ungodly Things (2002)

Make no mistake. Christ can use all manner of circumstances, unmet expectations, and disappointments to make us look up.

When you've stared at the face of Christ long enough through the lens of scripture, you will begin to look around you and see men clearly.

So Long, Insecurity (2010)

MOTHER TERESA

Born in 1910 in modern-day Macedonia, as a child Anjeze Gonxhe Bojaxhiu was fascinated by tales of missionaries and decided that was what she wanted to be when she grew up. At eighteen she joined the Sisters of Loreto, choosing to be named after Therese of Lisieux but adopting the Spanish spelling, Teresa.

While teaching in Calcutta she became increasingly distressed by the poverty, hunger, and violence she saw. Then she experienced the "call within a call" that prompted her to leave the convent and live and work among the poor.

Despite many fears and temptations, she founded the Missionaries of Charity and spent the rest of her life caring for the sick and the dying.

In 1979 she was awarded the Nobel Peace Prize, and the Catholic Church has begun the process of proclaiming her a saint. She died in 1997 in Calcutta.

✍

The greatest destroyer of peace is abortion because if a mother can kill her own child, what is left but for me to kill you and you to kill me? There is nothing between.

Nobel Peace Prize Lecture (1979)

We are taught from the very first moment to discover Christ under the distressing disguise of the poor, the sick, the outcasts. Christ presents Himself to us under every disguise: the dying, the paralytic, the leper, the invalid, the orphan.

It is impossible to love God without loving our neighbor.

Loving Jesus (1991)

In the silence of the heart God speaks. If you face God in prayer and silence, God will speak to you. Then you will know that you are nothing. It is only when you realize your nothingness, your emptiness, that God can fill you with Himself. Souls of prayer are souls of great silence.

In the Heart of the World: Thoughts, Stories and Prayers (2010)

I would rather make mistakes in kindness and compassion than work miracles in unkindness and hardness.

A Gift for God: Prayers and Meditations (2003)

The greatest disease in the West today is not tuberculosis or leprosy; it is being unwanted, unloved, and uncared for. We can cure physical diseases with medicine, but the only cure for loneliness, despair, and hopelessness is love. There are many in the world who are dying for a piece of bread but there are many more dying for a little love. The poverty in the West is a different kind of poverty—it is not only a poverty of loneliness but also of spirituality. There's a hunger for love, as there is a hunger for God.

A Simple Path: Mother Teresa (1995)

MURRAY, ANDREW

Andrew Murray was born in South Africa in 1828 but educated in Scotland. He then went to Holland to be ordained by the Dutch Reformed Church. Back in South Africa he pastored four different churches, becoming a prime mover in the revival of 1860.

He was a founding member of the South Africa General Mission, which grew beyond the borders of South Africa and became the Africa Evangelical Fellowship. Later that fellowship amalgamated with SIM (originally the Soudan Interior Mission) and continues to support missionaries in Africa and Asia to this day.

Andrew Murray died in 1917 in Wellington, South Africa.

His books include *Abide in Christ, Absolute Surrender, God's Will: Our Dwelling Place, Thy Will Be Done,* and *Waiting on God.*

✍

It is a grand thing to have a man with whom God is, to entrust one's business to.

There are many who have accepted Christ as their Lord, but have never yet come to the final, absolute surrender of everything.

If there is any trouble in your heart, if you are in darkness, or in the power of sin, I bring to you the Son of God, with the promise that He will come in and take charge.

The Spirit of God is a holy spirit and His work is to make free from the power of sin and death.

I have nothing but God; I trust God; I am waiting upon God; my flesh rests in Him; I have given up everything, that I may rest, waiting upon what God is to do to me.

Our glorious, exalted, almighty, ever present Christ! Why is it that you and I cannot trust Him fully, perfectly to do His work?

Humility is one of the great marks of a crucified man.

Ah, I believe that the Church of Christ suffers more today from trusting in intellect, in sagacity, in culture, and in mental refinement, than from almost anything else.

May it please God to reveal to His children the nearness of Christ standing and knocking at the door of every heart, ready to come in and rest forever there and to lead the soul into His rest.

I cannot die for sin like Christ, but I can and I must die to sin like Christ. Christ died for me. In that He stands alone. Christ died to sin, and in that I have fellowship with Him.

Master's Indwelling (1895)

Work is not done for its own sake. Its value consists in the object it attains. The purpose of Him who commands or performs the work gives it its real worth.

The true Christian is one who knows God's power working in himself, and finds it his true joy to have the very life of God flow into him, and through him, and out from him to those around.

Let the Church awake to her calling to train the feeblest of her members to know that Christ counts upon every redeemed one to live wholly for His work. This alone is true Christianity, is full salvation.

The great majority of those who are counted believers are doing nothing towards making Christ known to their fellowmen.

Christ counted it no humiliation to be able to do nothing of Himself, to be always and absolutely dependent on the Father.

An intense desire to be cleansed from every sin lies at the root of fitness for true service.

He that would truly work for God must follow after holiness.

When the believer does not know that Christ is living in him, does not know the Spirit and power of God working in him, there may be much earnestness and diligence, with little that lasts for eternity.

Faith opens the eyes to see the blessedness of God's service, the sufficiency of the strength provided, and the rich reward.

This is the one purpose of God, the great worker in heaven, the source and master of all work, that the glory of His love and power and blessing may be shown.

Working for God (1901)

The deeper our despair of entering aright into the thoughts of God, the greater the confidence of expectancy may be. God wants to make His Word true in us.

But Eve was led astray by the desire for knowledge—"the fruit was to be desired to make one wise"—and man got a knowledge of good without possessing it, a knowledge of it only from the evil that was its opposite. And since that day man has ever sought his religion more in knowledge than in life.

Let not the understanding, but the whole heart set upon the living God as the teacher, be the chief thing, when thou enterest thy closet. Then shalt thou find good understanding. God will give thee an understanding heart, a spiritual understanding.

There is a secret feeling that all this brings more sacrifice, difficulty, and danger, than we are ready for. This is only true as long as we have not seen how absolute God's claim is, how unutterably blessed it is to yield to it, and how certain that God Himself will work it in us.

The only proof of true, living, saving knowledge of God; the only proof of not being self-deceived in our religion; of God's love not being an imagination, but a possession, is, keeping His Word.

The blessedness and the blessing of God's Word is only to be known by doing it.

It was especially the desire for knowledge, in a way and at a time God had forbidden it, that led Eve astray. As the outcome of the temptation, to think that we can take the knowledge of God's truth for ourselves out of His Word as we will, is still our greatest danger.

Bow before the mercy seat. There the consciousness of your unworthiness will not hinder you, but be a real help in trusting God. There you may have the assured confidence that your upward look will be met by His eye, that your prayer can be heard, that His loving answer will be given.

That intellect is most needful, to offer to the heart the Word of God which the Holy Spirit can quicken. And yet it is absolutely impotent, either to impart, or quicken, the true life. It is but a servant that carries the food: it is the heart that must feed, and be nourished and live.

Through the will of God, delighted in, and done, lies our only way to the heart of God, His only way to our heart. Keep the commandments. This is the way to every blessing.

You are in danger of substituting prayer and Bible study for living fellowship with God, the living interchange of giving Him your love, your heart, your life, and receiving from Him His love, His life, His Spirit. Your needs and their expression, your desire to pray humbly and earnestly and believingly may so occupy you, that the light of His countenance and the joy of His love cannot enter you.

All the infinities of God and the eternal world dwell in the Word as the seed of eternal life. And as the full-grown oak is so mysteriously greater than the acorn from which it springs, so God's words are but seeds from which God's mighty wonders of grace can grow up.

Prayer's Inner Chamber (1912)

It is a great thing to enter the inner chamber, and shut the door, and meet the Father in secret. It is a greater thing to open the door again, and go out, in an enjoyment of that presence which nothing can disturb.

A prayerful spirit is the spirit to which God will speak. A prayerful spirit will be a listening spirit waiting to hear what God says.

Count upon God, who has seen thee in secret, to reward thee openly, to give grace in dealings with men to maintain thy communion with Him, and to make them know His grace and light are on thee.

What a nobility would come into life if secret prayer were not only an asking for some new sense of comfort, or light, or strength, but the giving way of life just for one day into the sure and safe keeping of a mighty and faithful God.

In prayer man rises to heaven to dwell with God: in the Word God comes to dwell with man. In prayer man gives himself to God: in the Word God gives Himself to man.

The highest blessedness of prayer will be our ceasing to pray, to let God speak.

The Prayer Life (1912)

The omniscience of God is a wonder. The omnipotence of God is a wonder. God's spotless holiness is a wonder. None of these things can we understand. But the greatest wonder of all is the mercy of God.

God desires nothing from you but that you should really acknowledge your sin and cast yourself down before Him as a guilty sinner. Then you will certainly and speedily receive His grace.

Always meet with God as a God who desires truth in the inward parts. In all your confession of sin, in all your religion, in your whole existence, let truth in the inward parts be your desire, as it is the desire of God.

Do not forget that the aim God has in view in His grace and your redemption is to restore the broken bond of fellowship and love between Him and the sinner. True religion consists in this, that the soul should find its highest happiness in personal communication with God.

Since God Himself is a steadfast Rock, the foundation of all certitude and steadfastness, it must be by faith or holding fast to God that man can become steadfast.

Have Mercy upon Me (1896)

NEE, WATCHMAN

Seventeen-year-old Watchman Nee, who was born in Shantou, China, in 1903, wasn't interested in religion until his mother returned from a revival meeting and apologized for punishing him unjustly. Impressed, he attended the next meeting.

Hearing Christ's call, Nee enrolled in a Bible institute but was dismissed for laziness. A period of illness followed during which he felt God explaining His plan more clearly. Watchman went on to establish the tradition of home churches in China, wrote extensively, and held many conferences. After the Communists came to power, he was arrested and spent the last twenty years of his life in jail. Only his wife, Charity, was allowed to visit him.

Watchman died in 1972.

His books include *The Spiritual Man*, *The Breaking of the Outer Man and the Releasing of the Spirit*, *What Shall This Man Do?*, and *Love Not the World*.

✍

Strong-willed people are convinced their feelings, ways, and judgments are always right.

Anyone who serves God will discover sooner or later that the great hindrance to his work is not others but himself.

The Release of the Spirit (1965)

There is nothing in our lives that is accidental. Every day's happenings are measured by the Lord.

Do not linger in the shame of sin as if such suffering will bring in holiness.

Not I but Christ (1948)

We cannot expect a tailor to make us a coat if we do not give him any cloth, nor a builder to build us a house if we let him have no building material; and in just the same way we cannot expect the Lord to live out His life in us if we do not give Him our lives in which to live.

You will recognize the will of God and you will find that that is what your heart delights in alone. You will no longer even shed a tear in sympathy with the flesh.

Normal Christian Life (c. 1935)

Those who know God have no need to protect their rights. Because they believe in Him, they learn to bear the Cross daily and to rely upon Him for the outcome.

When we are defeated and God does not speak, He is leading us to the end of ourselves and to a complete confidence in Him.

Changed into His Likeness (1967)

OGILVIE, LLOYD JOHN

Born in Kenosha, Wisconsin, in 1930, Lloyd John Ogilvie later became the sixty-first chaplain of the US Senate. Since the early days of his ministry, he has focused on counseling and helping leaders in society and industry, believing them best placed to improve the situations of others.

He was chaplain to leaders in the steel industry during his time in Pennsylvania and to the movers and shakers of the movie industry during his time in Hollywood. He believes that listening is the key to effective communication and shapes his books and broadcasts to the most urgent questions of society.

In 1996, Baylor University named him one of the twelve most effective preachers in the English-speaking world.

His books include *If I Should Wake before I Die*; *Ask Him Anything*; *If God Cares, Why Do I Still Have Problems?*; and *The Red Ember in the White Ash*.

Reaching one person at a time is still the best way to reach the world.

To be in Christ is to be in ministry and to be in ministry is to communicate to people the joy and power of the new life in Christ.

Life without Limits (1975)

What if God was only faithful when He felt like it, only dependable part of the time, only loving on special occasions? Thank goodness, He is always faithful to His own nature. The world desperately needs to see that same kind of faithfulness in our lives.

You can never be "good enough" on your own to please God. Only the Holy Spirit has what it takes to give us what it takes to please God: His essential goodness reproduced in us.

The Magnificent Vision (1980)

As long as we're in search of ourselves and our true identity, we will be under pressure.

People who hide aspects of their lives end up being fearful, often in areas unrelated to what they are hiding.

The Bush Is Still Burning (1980)

OMARTIAN, STORMIE

Stormie Sherk was born in 1952 in Brentwood, Tennessee. An abusive childhood led her into a period of rebellion. While she was working as a dancer, singer, and actress, a friend in the entertainment industry introduced her to the remedy for her pain: Jesus. Thereafter she began experiencing the power of prayer and the love of the Lord, experiences that would touch others through her many books.

Stormie and her husband, Michael Omartian, have written many praise and worship songs together. She has written over fifty books and regularly tops the Christian bestseller lists.

Her books include *The Power of a Praying Wife; The Power of a Praying Husband; Stormie: A Story of Forgiveness and Healing;* and *Lord, I Want to Be Whole: The Power of Prayer and Scripture in Emotional Healing.*

People who say the Bible isn't relevant today obviously don't know the Author.

The hardest part about letting God fight your battle is that He sometimes waits until the eleventh hour so you will have no doubt of where the power is coming from.

Just Enough Light for the Step I'm On (1999)

Let go of as many expectations as possible. . .instead, ask God to make any necessary changes.

The Power of a Praying Wife (1997)

ORTBERG, JOHN

John Ortberg, who was born in 1957 in Rockford, Illinois, is the senior pastor at Menlo Park Presbyterian Church. His preaching emphasizes spiritual transformation and the possibility of becoming less earthly and more spiritual through encounters with God. He teaches that the material things of the world blind us to our true desire, which is for eternity with the Father.

He preaches and writes with subtle touches of humor, using everyday experiences to get his messages across. He is a regular speaker at Promise Keepers conferences and Global Leadership Summits.

His books include *If You Want to Walk on Water, You've Got to Get Out of the Boat*; *Everybody's Normal Till You Get to Know Them*; *When the Game Is Over, It All Goes Back in the Box*; and *Who Is This Man? The Unpredictable Impact of the Inescapable Jesus*.

🖎

Acceptance is an act of the heart. To accept someone is to affirm to them that you think it's a very good thing they are alive.

There is a world of difference between being friendly to someone because they're useful to you and being someone's friend.

Everybody's Normal Till You Get to Know Them (2003)

Our beliefs are not just estimates of probabilities. They are also the instruments that guide our actions.

Faith involves certain beliefs. Faith involves an attitude of hope and confidence. But at its core, faith is trusting a person.

Faith and Doubt (2008)

At the deepest level, pride is the choice to exclude both God and other people from their rightful place in our hearts. Jesus said the essence of the spiritual life is to love God and to love people. Pride destroys our capacity to love.

Following Jesus simply means learning from Him how to arrange my life around activities that enable me to live in the fruit of the Spirit.

The Life You've Always Wanted (2002)

Never try to have more faith—just get to know God better. And because God is faithful, the better you know Him, the more you'll trust Him.

We are to worship God, not because His ego needs it, but because without worship, our experience and enjoyment of God are not complete. We worship God not so much because He needs it, but because we do.

If You Want to Walk on Water, You've Got to Get Out of the Boat (2001)

I cannot force God to give me the guidance or help I think I need. There may be a good reason for His remaining silent sometimes.

Once you see God in an ordinary moment at an ordinary place, you never know where He'll show up next.

God Is Closer Than You Think (2005)

God did not create us out of need. He created us out of His love.

Love beyond Reason (1998)

Born in 1616 in Stadhampton, England, John Owen was a church leader and member of the British Parliament during the time of Oliver Cromwell. His speech calling for sincerity in religion from those in high places attracted the admiration and friendship of Cromwell, who found him a position at Trinity College in Dublin before making him vice-chancellor of Oxford University.

After Cromwell died, Owen was deprived of his position and retired to work on his books. King Charles II gave him one hundred guineas to alleviate his suffering, and he used some of it to have John Bunyan (author of *The Pilgrim's Progress*) released from jail.

Owen died in 1683 in Ealing, England.

His written works include *Communion with God*, *The Glory of Christ*, and *A Dissertation on Divine Justice*.

☞

The vigor, and power, and comfort of our spiritual life depends on the mortification of the deeds of the flesh.

Spiritually sick men cannot sweat out their distemper with working.

A man may easier see without eyes, speak without tongue, than truly mortify one sin without the Spirit.

There is no death of sin without the death of Christ.

Set faith at work on Christ for the killing of your sin.

The mortification of indwelling sin remaining in our mortal bodies, that it may not have life and power to bring forth the works or deeds of the flesh, is the constant duty of believers.

Do you mortify; do you make it your daily work; be always at it while you live; cease not a day from this work; be killing sin or it will be killing you.

Sin will not only be striving, acting, rebelling, troubling, disquieting, but if let alone, if not continually mortified, it will bring forth great, cursed, scandalous, soul-destroying sins.

Sin aims always at the utmost; every time it rises up to tempt or entice, may it have its own course, it would go out to the utmost sin in that kind.

Of the Mortification of Sin in Believers (1656)

PACKER, J. I.

Born in 1926 in Gloucester, England, to a railway clerk and his wife, James Innell Packer went on to become one of the most influential evangelicals in North America.

As a student in Oxford, he got to hear lectures by C. S. Lewis that would alter the course of his life. He became a priest in 1953, lecturing and preaching in several English colleges before moving to Vancouver, where he became professor of theology at Regent College. He is a frequent contributor to *Christianity Today* and serves as its executive editor.

His books include *Knowing God*, *The Anglican Identity Problem*, *Meeting God*, and *Affirming the Apostles' Creed*.

✍

Christ's command means that we all should be devoting all our resources of ingenuity and enterprise to the task of making the gospel known in every possible way to every possible person.

The gospel starts by teaching us that we, as creatures, are absolutely dependent on God, and that He, as Creator, has an absolute claim on us. Only when we have learned this can we see what sin is, and only when we see what sin is can we understand the good news of salvation from sin.

Evangelism and the Sovereignty of God (2008)

Adoption is a family idea, conceived in terms of love, and viewing God as father.

One can know a great deal about godliness without much knowledge of God.

Knowing God (1993)

PALAU, LUIS

Luis Palau was born in 1934 in Buenos Aires, Argentina. His father died when he was ten years old. Two years later, he gave his life to Jesus. A Billy Graham broadcast inspired Palau, and he soon began working for Graham as a translator. Later Graham would help Palau set up his own ministry.

He arrived in the United States in 1960 to attend Multnomah Bible College and became a citizen two years later. His conventions attract many thousands of people, and he is particularly popular with the younger audience. It has been suggested he might be the natural successor to his friend and mentor, Billy Graham.

His books include *Where Is God When Bad Things Happen?*, *What to Do When You Don't Want to Go to Church*, *God Is Relevant*, and *A Friendly Dialogue between an Atheist and a Christian*.

✍

God isn't impressed in the least by job title, bank account, or standing in the community. God is searching for a servant's heart.

Impatience. How many of us have ruined rare and unusual opportunities to serve Christ because of impatience? It doesn't seem like such a big thing and yet—do you know what impatience represents? It is a sign of distrust in the sovereign control of God.

Heart after God (1978)

No matter how great our burdens or how deep our pain, God is able to comfort us. No matter how severe the pressures of daily life, they can't separate us from the tenderness and compassion of our Heavenly Father. When we allow God to comfort us, His power and grace are magnified. Then God can equip us to comfort others and introduce them to our all-sufficient Father.

Stop Pretending (2003)

Sadly, even many committed Christians struggle to know how Jesus can truly transform their lives. Even "strong believers" have doubts, concerns, and unresolved worries. Deep down, when everything is quiet, they truly wonder how it all plays out.

Changed by Faith: Trust God with Your Broken Pieces. . .and Watch What Happens (with Jay Fordice, 2011)

Born in 1623 in Auvergne, France, Blaise Pascal was a child prodigy and, later, a polymath, being an innovative thinker in many disciplines. He was a follower of the Catholic sect of Jansenism, which emphasized original sin and predestination. Because of the perceived similarity with Calvinism, the pope declared much of Jansenism to be heretical.

His initial enthusiasm for religion waned for a number of years but returned after a vision, which he wrote down and stitched into the lining of every jacket he wore thereafter.

His *Pensées*, or *Thoughts*, were compiled from papers found after his death in 1662 and have since been declared a masterwork of literature, spiritual and otherwise.

His books (dealing with faith) also include *The Provincial Letters*.

☞

People are generally better persuaded by the reasons they themselves have discovered than by those which have come into the mind of others.

To carry piety to the point of superstition is to destroy it.

I can have only compassion for those who sincerely bewail their doubt, who regard it as the greatest of misfortunes, and who, sparing no effort to escape it, make of this inquiry their principal and most serious occupations.

I would have far more fear of being mistaken, and of finding that the Christian religion was true, than of not being mistaken in believing it true.

Nothing is so important to man as his own state, nothing is as formidable as his eternity; and thus it is not natural that there should be men indifferent to the loss of their existence and the perils of everlasting suffering.

It concerns all our life to know whether the soul may be mortal or immortal.

Faith is different from proof; the one is human, the other is gift of God.

If man is not made for God, why is he not happy except in God? If man is made for God, why is he so opposed to God?

Knowledge of God without knowledge of our wretchedness makes for pride.

Between us and heaven or hell there is only life, which is the frailest thing in the world.

That passion may not harm us, let us act as if we had only eight hours to live.

It is deplorable to see everybody deliberating only about the means, never the end.

It is superstition to put one's hope in formalities; but it is pride to be unwilling to submit to them.

We should seek the truth without hesitation; and, if we refuse it, we show that we value the esteem of men more than the search for truth.

Contradiction is a poor sign of truth. Many certain things are contradicted. Many false things pass without contradiction.

Pensées (translated by Roger Ariew) (c. 1660)

PHILLIPS, J. B.

John Bertram Phillips was born in 1906 in Barnes, England. In 1930 he was ordained as an Anglican clergyman in the Church of England. When preaching to the children of his church's youth club, he often found that they struggled to understand the language of scripture.

During World War II, when London was being bombed, Phillips and his youngsters often had to spend days and nights in air-raid shelters. He took advantage of the forced periods of inactivity to translate the book of Colossians and, eventually, the rest of the New Testament into language young people could understand. With the help of Christian author and apologist C. S. Lewis, his "translation" was published after the war ended.

Phillips died in 1982.

His books include *The New Testament in Modern English*, *The Ring of Truth: A Translator's Testimony*, and *God Our Contemporary*.

No figure in history, however splendid and memorable, can possibly satisfy the mind which is seeking the living contemporary God.

There are undoubtedly professing Christians with childish conceptions of God which could not stand up to the winds of real life for five minutes.

Your God Is Too Small (1952)

PIPER, JOHN

Born in 1946 in Chattanooga, Tennessee, John Stephen Piper is the son of a traveling evangelist and church planter. He originally intended to study pre-med at college but changed his mind during a period of illness. Instead, he studied for a bachelor of divinity qualification at Fuller Theological Seminary. There Daniel Fuller, the son of the college founder, introduced Piper to the works of Jonathan Edwards, which had a significant impact on his life.

In 1994 Piper began his Desiring God Ministries, a foundation that makes all of his books and sermons available for free online, as well as sells CDs and DVDs. The philosophy behind Desiring God Ministries is one of passion for the supremacy of God in all things.

His many books include *The Supremacy of God in Preaching*, *Recovering Biblical Manhood and Womanhood*, *The Supremacy of Christ in a Postmodern World*, and *The Pastor as Scholar and the Scholar as Pastor*.

✍

Since Christ is the incarnate display of the wealth of the mercies of God, it is not surprising that His life on earth was a lavish exhibit of mercies to all kinds of people. Every kind of need and pain was touched by the mercies of Jesus in His few years on earth.

Christ does not exist in order to make much of us. We exist in order to enjoy making much of Him.

Seeing and Savoring Jesus Christ (2004)

The world is not impressed when Christians get rich and say thanks to God. They are impressed when God is so satisfying that we give our riches away for Christ's sake and count it gain.

Idleness does not grow in the soil of fellowship with God. God created us for work so that by consciously relying on His power and consciously shaping the world after His excellence, we might be satisfied in Him, and He might be glorified in us.

Don't Waste Your Life (2003)

Satan is not mainly interested in causing us misery. He is mainly interested in making Christ look bad. He hates Christ. And he hates the glory of Christ. He will do all he can to keep people from seeing Christ as glorious.

The glory of God is the beautiful brightness of God. There is no greater brightness. Nothing in the universe, nor in the imagination of any man or angel, is brighter than the brightness of God.

God Is the Gospel (2005)

God created us to enjoy Him because joy is the clearest witness to the worth of what we enjoy. It's the deepest reverberation in the heart of man of the value of God's glory.

The Supremacy of Christ in a Postmodern World (2007)

Nothing keeps God at the center of our worship like the biblical conviction that the essence of worship is deep, heartfelt satisfaction in Him and the conviction that the pursuit of satisfaction is why we are together.

The great hindrance to worship is not that we are pleasure-seeking people, but that we are willing to settle for such pitiful pleasures.

The Dangerous Duty of Delight (2001)

The ultimate question is not who you are but whose you are.

There is no autonomy in the fallen world. We are governed by sin or governed by God.

The Passion of Jesus Christ (2004)

The Word of God is not a dead word or an ineffective word. It has life in it. And because it has life in it, it produces effects.

There is something about the Truth, as God revealed it, that connects it to God as a source of all life and power. God loves His Word. He is partial to His Word. He honors His Word with His presence and power.

Pierced by the Word (2003)

REDMAN, MATT

Matthew (Matt) Redman is an English singer, songwriter, and worship leader. He has won two Grammy awards for his song "10,000 Reasons," and many other Christian singers and bands have recorded his songs.

Born in 1974 in Chorleywood, England, while still in his mid-teens Redman was performing live as a worship leader at the Soul Survivor festivals in England. He has recorded eleven praise albums (and many other "event" albums) and written books on his worship experiences.

His better-known songs include "Blessed Be Your Name," "God of This City," "You Never Let Go," and "Heart of Worship." His books include *The Unquenchable Worshipper*, *The Heart of Worship Files*, *Blessed Be Your Name* (with his wife, Beth Redman), and *Mirror Ball*.

We may have faith to believe in God as Lord of the calm—but do we also have faith to believe in Him as Lord of the storm?

In our darkest times, we must proclaim Jesus as the One who is powerful enough to heal and merciful enough to rescue. But all the time, underneath must be a conviction that even if for some reason we are not relieved of our struggle, our worship will not falter.

Blessed Be Your Name (2005)

The heart posture of humility recognizes that God alone can do powerful and meaningful things. By His grace we may get involved with such ministry, but we are ever the carriers and never the cause.

Creativity is essential when it comes to our congregational worship. It's a sign of abundant life.

Inside Out Worship (2005)

Trust is a beautiful and costly act of worship—an honoring response to the sovereignty of God and to His fatherly heart.

The most meaningful and powerful worship always comes at a price—the whole of our lives placed on His altar.

Facedown (2004)

The more we see of Jesus, the more we know there's still so much to be seen. The more He touches our lives, the more we realize our desperate need for Him to consume every part of us.

The heart of God loves the offerings of a persevering worshipper. Though overwhelmed by many troubles, they are even more overwhelmed by the beauty of God.

The Unquenchable Worshipper (2001)

RYLE, J. C.

John Charles Ryle was the first Anglican bishop of Liverpool in England. Born in 1816 in Macclesfield, England, to a wealthy banker, he was heading for a career in politics when a sermon on Ephesians 2 turned his life around.

During a thirty-eight-year stint as parish priest, he became one of England's leading evangelicals. He was appointed to the Liverpool Bishopric at the suggestion of Prime Minister Benjamin Disraeli.

His assertive but friendly style of preaching won him the support of many blue-collar workers. During his time in Liverpool, he established over forty churches. He died in Liverpool in 1900.

His written works include *Christian Leaders of the Last Century*; *Light from Old Times, or Protestant Facts and Men*; and *Expository Thoughts on Matthew, Mark, Luke, and John.*

It is always unpleasant to be spoken against, and forsaken, and lied about, and to stand alone. But there is no help for it. The cup which our Master drank must be drunk by His disciples.

I grant freely that it costs little to be a mere outward Christian.

To be a Christian it will cost a man his love of ease.

A cheap Christianity, without a cross, will prove in the end a useless Christianity, without a crown.

Many would save themselves much sorrow and trouble if they would only remember the question, "What does it cost?"

No doubt Christ's way to eternal life is a way of pleasantness. But it is folly to shut our eyes to the fact that His way is narrow, and the cross comes before the crown.

The presence and company of Christ will make amends for all we suffer here below.

The time present, no doubt, is not a time of ease. It is a time of watching and praying, fighting and struggling, believing and working. But it is only for a few years.

Our sins are often as dear to us as our children: we love them, hug them, cleave to them, and delight in them. To part with them is as hard as cutting off a right hand, or plucking out a right eye.

Surely these are times when we ought often to sit down and "count the cost," and to consider the state of our souls.

Holiness, Its Nature, Hindrances, Difficulties, and Roots (c. 1850)

Death, and judgment, and eternity are not fancies, but stern realities. Make time to think about them. Stand still, and look them in the face. You will be obliged one day to make time to die, whether you are prepared or not.

Next to the office of him who ministers to men's souls, there is none really more useful and honorable than that of him who ministers to the soul's frail tabernacle—the body.

It is easy to sneer at the simple facts and doctrines of Christianity, and to talk great swelling words about "mind," and "thought," and "intellect," and "reason." But there is no getting over the broad fact that it is the body and not the mind, and the wants of the body, by which the world is governed.

The restless, high-pressure hurry in which men live endangers the very foundations of personal religion.

He that endeavors to check disease, to alleviate suffering, to lessen pain, to help the self-curative powers of nature, and to lengthen life, may surely take comfort in the thought, that, however much he may fail, he is at any rate walking in the footsteps of Jesus of Nazareth.

The Church, which only cares for saving souls, and the State, which only cares for educating minds, are both making a vast mistake.

Too often they marry in haste and repent at leisure, and lay up misery for life by wedding an uncongenial partner.

Do nothing rashly. What are you doing? Where are you going? What will be the end and consequence of your present line of action? Stop and think. By thoughtless actions they created habits which have become second nature to them.

It was the precious lifeblood, which flowed from our Lord's crucified body on Calvary, which purchased for us redemption from the curse of a broken law.

Resolve by the grace of God, if you love life, that you will have regular seasons for examining yourself, and looking over the accounts of your soul.

The Upper Room (c. 1880)

The only true wisdom is to be always prepared to meet God, to put nothing off which concerns eternity and to live like men ready to depart at any moment.

Expository Thoughts on the Gospels (1879)

A day is coming upon us all when the value of everything will be altered.

Practical Religion (1878)

RYRIE, CHARLES

Born in 1925 in Alton, Illinois, Charles Caldwell Ryrie is the editor of the *Ryrie Study Bible*, to which he has contributed more than ten thousand explanatory notes. Since the book's first publication by Moody Publishing in 1978, it has sold over two million copies.

Charles Ryrie has degrees from Haverford College, Dallas Theological Seminary, University of Edinburgh, and Liberty Baptist Theological Seminary. He has served as professor of systematic theology, dean of doctoral studies at Dallas Theological Seminary, and professor at what is now Cairn University. He has frequently contributed to *Bibliotheca Sacra*, the journal of Dallas Theological Seminary.

His books include *Transformed by His Glory*, *Nailing Down a Board: Serving Effectively on the Not-for-Profit Board*, *The Basis of Premillennial Faith*, and *Neo-orthodoxy*.

✍

Conversion brings with it a new capacity with which we may now serve God and righteousness. Before salvation, we were servants of sin, but now we may be servants of righteousness. The unsaved man has only one capacity, but the Christian has two.

The mercies of God, the basis for our dedication, are far greater than those of any human master, and the blessings of a life dedicated in service to God are far more certain in their richness. Why so many hesitate to dedicate themselves to Him is difficult to understand.

Balancing the Christian Life (1969)

SCHAEFFER, EDITH

Born to missionaries in Wenzhou, China, in 1914, Edith Seville also had a Chinese name that translated as "Beautiful Happiness." She completed her formal education in Pennsylvania, where she met Francis Schaeffer, her future husband.

In 1955 Edith and Francis established L'Abri, a community in Switzerland that sought to answer the questions of those seeking honest, satisfying answers to questions of life and faith.

Her book *Affliction*, which addresses human suffering in faith terms, won a Gold Medallion Award from the Evangelical Christian Publishers Association. In 2000 Edith Schaeffer was included in Helen Kooiman Hosier's book *100 Christian Women Who Changed the Twentieth Century*.

She passed away in 2013 in Gryon, Switzerland.

Her books include *Affliction*, *What Is a Family?*, *Common Sense Christian Living*, *10 Things Parents Must Teach Their Children—and Learn Themselves*, and *A Celebration of Children*.

✍

God is utterly fair.

Life without God. Senseless? Meaningless? Full of despair? Yes.

Common Sense Christian Living (1983)

Being able to think, have ideas, and then to choose to make or do something, is essential to creativity.

Constructive creativity not only affects other human beings, but brings glory to God by being in the stream of His creativity.

What Is a Family? (1975)

SCHAEFFER, FRANCIS

Born in Germantown, Pennsylvania, in 1912, Francis August Schaeffer was a Christian philosopher, church leader, and founder of the L'Abri community. L'Abri (meaning "the Shelter") was a chalet in Switzerland where people could study and ask questions about faith. It currently has study centers in seven other countries.

He is often credited with helping the Protestant evangelical movement reengage with political issues in the late seventies and early eighties.

Schaeffer died of lymphoma in 1984, but L'Abri, the Francis A. Schaeffer

Foundation, and the Francis A. Schaeffer Institute carry on his work.

His books include *True Spirituality*, *The God Who Is There*, *He Is There and He Is Not Silent*, *No Final Conflict*, and *Genesis in Space and Time*.

If there is no absolute moral standard, then one cannot say in a final sense that anything is right or wrong.

If there is no absolute beyond man's ideas, then there is no final appeal to judge between individuals and groups whose moral judgments conflict. We are merely left with conflicting opinions.

How Should We Then Live? (1976)

All men bear the image of God. They have value not because they are redeemed, but because they are God's creation in God's image.

The Mark of the Christian (1970)

It is only as we consciously bring each victory to His feet, and keep it there as we think of it—and especially as we speak of it—that we can avoid the pride of that victory, which can be worse than the sin over which we claim to have had the victory.

True Spirituality (1971)

SHELDON, CHARLES

Charles Monroe Sheldon, born in Wellsville, New York, in 1857, was a Congregational minister and advocate of Christian Socialism. He was less interested in doctrinal definitions of what it took to be saved and more interested in the practicalities of living a life as he believed Jesus would. It was while preaching at the Congregational Church of Topeka, Kansas, that he developed the concept "What would Jesus do?"—addressing practical, everyday issues in a Christlike way. His idea took off. After being asked to write a column for the *Topeka Daily Capital* along the same lines, his columns increased the paper's circulation so much that their printing presses couldn't keep up.

Charles Sheldon was a prohibitionist, a vegetarian, and a supporter of equal rights for both sexes and all races. He died in 1946 in Topeka, Kansas.

His books include *In His Steps: What Would Jesus Do?* and *The High Calling*.

✍

O Lord! how long shall Christian people continue to support, by their silence and their ballots, the greatest form of slavery now known in America?

The environment does have a good deal to do with the character.

No man can tell until he is moved by the Divine Spirit what he may do, or how he may change the current of a lifetime of fixed habits of thought and speech and action.

We must be free from fanaticism on one hand and too much caution on the other.

After we have asked the Spirit to tell us what Jesus would do and have received an answer to it, we are to act regardless of the results to ourselves.

Our motto will be, "What would Jesus do?" Our aim will be to act just as He would if He were in our palaces, regardless of immediate results.

The moral side of every political question will be considered its most important side, and the ground will be distinctly taken that nations, as well as individuals, are under the same law, to do all things to the glory of God, as the first rule of action.

There are times when a sermon has a value and power due to conditions in the audience rather than to anything new or startling or eloquent in the words or the arguments presented.

It is easy to love an individual sinner, especially if he is personally picturesque, or interesting. To love a multitude of sinners, lay distinctly a Christlike quality.

No young man can live in such an atmosphere of unpunished dishonesty and lawlessness, without wrecking his character.

In His Steps (1896)

SIMPSON, A. B.

Born in 1843, Albert Benjamin Simpson was raised in a strict Presbyterian (almost Puritan) family on Prince Edward Island in Canada. At age thirty he began preaching in America: first in Kentucky and then in New York City. While he was in New York, his heart was drawn to the great number of poor immigrants arriving in the city. His church had other priorities, though, so he left it and founded the Gospel Tabernacle, where all would be welcome.

Working with so many people from other countries eventually led him to think about spreading the Gospel outside the United States, which inspired him to found the Christian and Missionary Alliance. He was also the instigator of the "Fourfold Gospel" concept, wherein Christ is seen as Savior, Sanctifier, Healer, and coming King. He lived until 1919.

Be brave. Cowards always get hurt. Brave men generally come out unharmed.

When God wants to bring more power into our lives, He brings more pressure. He is generating spiritual force by friction.

Every spiritual habit begins with difficulty and effort and watchfulness.

The smallest grain of faith is a deathless and incorruptible germ which will yet plant the heavens and cover the earth with harvests of imperishable glory.

It is all right when God sends us the approval of our fellow men; however, we must never make that approval a motive in our life.

Every fear is distrust, and trust is the remedy for fear.

Perils as well as privileges attend the higher Christian life. The nearer we come to God, the thicker the hosts of darkness in heavenly places.

Have you ever learned the beautiful art of letting God take care of you and giving all your thought and strength to pray for others and for the kingdom of God? It will relieve you of a thousand cares.

Christ bids us live in an atmosphere of love.

We are the only light the world has. The Lord could come down Himself and give light to the world, but He has chosen differently.

Days of Heaven upon Earth (1897)

SLESSOR, MARY

Born in Gilcomston, Scotland, in 1848, Mary Slessor's father's drunkenness and the early deaths of her brothers forced her to work from an early age to save her family from poverty.

When she was twenty-seven she was inspired by tales of Scottish explorer and missionary David Livingstone and determined to follow his example. Supported by the Presbyterian Church's Missions Board, she sailed for Africa. The work ethic she developed as a child and her personal integrity would earn her the love and respect of the African people to whom she took the Gospel.

Except for visits home brought on by illness, Mary Slessor spent the remainder of her life in Africa, spreading the Gospel, promoting women's rights, saving abandoned babies, and preventing many tribal wars through her mediation. Her hero, David Livingstone, would later write in glowing terms about the ease with which she fit into the most difficult of situations.

She died in 1915 in Okoyong, Africa.

If I have done anything in my life it has been easy because the Master has gone before.

My life is one long daily, hourly, record of answered prayer.

You thought God was to hear and answer you by making everything straight and pleasant—not so are nations or churches or men and women born; not so is character made. God is answering your prayer in His way.

I know what it is to pray long years and never get the answer—I had to pray for my father. But I know my heavenly Father so well I can leave it with Him for the lower fatherhood.

Prayer is the greatest power God has put into our hands for service—praying is harder work than doing, at least I find it so.

Food is scarce just now. We live from hand to mouth. We have not more than will be our breakfast today, but I know we shall be fed, for God answers prayer.

Mary Slessor of Calabar, Fifth Phase IX (1917)

Smith, Hannah Whitall

Born in Germantown, Pennsylvania, in 1832, Hannah Whitall Smith was raised in a Quaker home. Later she was influenced by the Methodists and the Plymouth Brethren. She became heavily involved in the Holiness Movement, which taught that a life free from voluntary sin was possible through a second immersion in grace. She also supported the movement's sister organization in the United Kingdom called Higher Life. Mrs. Whitall Smith spoke regularly at meetings on both sides of the Atlantic and even traveled across Europe to spread the word. She was also a suffragist and a member of the Temperance Movement.

Her book *The Christian's Secret of a Happy Life* propelled her to celebrity status. She also wrote a spiritual autobiography entitled *The Unselfishness of God and How I Discovered It*. She died in 1911 in Iffley, England.

Foundations to be reliable must always be unshakable.

The Bible is a statement, not of theories, but of actual facts. . .things are not true because they are in the Bible, but they are only in the Bible because they are true.

If our hearts are full of our own wretched "I ams" we will have no ears to hear His glorious, soul-satisfying "I Am."

We must set our faces like a flint to believe, under each and every sorrow and trial, in the divine Comforter, and to accept and rejoice in His all-embracing comfort.

We must choose to be comforted.

A wavering Christian is a Christian who trusts in the love of God one day and doubts it the next, and who is alternately happy or miserable accordingly.

We are "God's workmanship," and God is good, therefore His workmanship must be good also; and we may securely trust that before He is done with us, He will make out of us something that will be to His glory, no matter how unlike this we may as yet feel ourselves to be.

Things we call good are often God's evil things, and our evil is His good. But, however things may look, we always know that God must give the best because He is God and could do no other.

Our lives are full of supposes. Suppose this should happen or suppose that should happen; but what could we do and how would we bear it? But, if we are living in the "high tower" of the dwelling place of God, all these supposes will drop out of our lives.

God's salvation is not a purchase to be made, nor wages to be earned, nor a summit to be climbed, nor a task to be accomplished; but it is simply and only a gift to be accepted, and can only be accepted by faith.

Before the acorn can bring forth the oak, it must become itself a wreck. No plant ever came from any but a wrecked seed.

We cannot drift from the love and care of an everlasting God.

The God of All Comfort (1906)

It is not what men do, that is the vital matter, but rather what they are.

Nothing so cultivates the grace of patience as the endurance of temptation.

Sight is not faith, and hearing is not faith, neither is feeling faith; but believing when we can neither see, hear, nor feel, is faith.

Man's part is to trust and God's part is to work.

Self must step aside, to let God work.

We must take our troubles to the Lord. . .but we must do more than that: we must leave them there.

Put together all the tenderest love you know of, multiply it by infinity, and you will begin to see glimpses of the love and grace of God.

The Christian's Secret of a Happy Life (1888)

SPROUL, R. C.

Born in 1939 in Pittsburgh, Pennsylvania, Robert Charles Sproul is a Calvinist theologian, author, and founder of Ligonier Ministries, an organization whose mission is to defend and proclaim the holiness of God. He hosts a daily radio broadcast called *Renewing Your Mind with R.C. Sproul*.

Having taught at numerous colleges and seminaries, Sproul went on to be senior minister of preaching and teaching at St. Andrew's Chapel in Sanford, Florida.

He served as editor for *The Reformation Study Bible* and has written over sixty books, including *The Donkey Who Carried a King*; *Unseen Realities: Heaven, Hell, Angels, and Demons*; *Can I Trust the Bible?*; and *How Should I Live in This World?*

✍

If a book has errors, it is not the Word of God. If a book is the Word of God, it does not have errors. We cannot have a book that is both the Word of God and errant.

I don't always feel His presence. But God's promises do not depend upon my feelings; they rest upon His integrity.

One Holy Passion (1987)

Christians get excited about the return of Jesus. Oh, happy day! Yes, it is a happy day for the saved, but for the unsaved the return of Jesus is the worst of all conceivable calamities.

Who needs a Savior when there's no clear and present threat of judgment?

Saved from What? (2002)

The Christ we believe, the Christ we trust, must be true if we are to be redeemed. A false Christ or substitute Christ cannot redeem. If it is thought unlikely that the biblical Christ can redeem, it is even less likely that the speculative Christ of human invention can redeem. Apart from the Bible we know nothing of consequence concerning the real Jesus. Ultimately our faith stands or falls with the biblical Jesus.

Following Christ (1991)

From brokenness to mission is the human pattern.

It's dangerous to assume that because a man is drawn to holiness in his study that he is thereby a holy man. I am sure that the reason that I have a deep hunger to learn of the holiness of God is precisely because I am not holy.

The Holiness of God (c. 1980)

Your job is to pray. My job is to bring about the result.

Themes from James (c. 2000)

The concept of the Trinity has emerged as a touchstone of truth, a nonnegotiable article of Christian orthodoxy. However, it has been a source of controversy throughout church history, and there remains much confusion about it to this day, with many people misunderstanding it in very serious ways.

In the Christian faith, all diversity finds its ultimate unity in God Himself, and it is significant that even in God's own being we find both unity and diversity—in fact in Him we find the ultimate ground for unity and diversity.

What Is the Trinity? (2011)

It is not a decision that converts a person; it is the power of the Holy Spirit that does so. We get into the kingdom not because we make a decision, walk down an aisle, raise a hand, or sign a card. We get into the kingdom because there is true faith in our hearts.

Can I Be Sure I'm Saved? (2010)

No person in history has provoked as much study, criticism, prejudice, or devotion as Jesus of Nazareth.

Unbelief is judged by Jesus not as an intellectual error but as a hostile act of prejudice against God Himself.

Who Is Jesus? (2009)

The triune God, who formed all things by His creative utterances and governs all things by His word of decree, made mankind in His own image for a life of communion with Himself, on the model of the eternal fellowship of loving communication within the Godhead.

When Adam fell, the Creator did not abandon mankind to final judgment but promised salvation and began to reveal Himself as Redeemer in a sequence of historical events centering on Abraham's family and culminating in the life, death, resurrection, present heavenly ministry, and promised return of Jesus Christ.

Can I Trust the Bible? (2009)

What is the goal of the Christian life? It is godliness born of obedience to Christ.

Obedience unlocks the riches of the Christian experience. Prayer prompts and nurtures obedience, putting the heart into the proper "frame of mind" to desire obedience.

Does Prayer Change Things? (2009)

No Christian can avoid theology. Every Christian has a theology. The issue, then, is not, do we want to have a theology? That's a given. The real issue is, do we have a *sound* theology? Do we embrace true or false doctrine?

Theology breeds controversies, no question about it.

Essential Truths of the Christian Faith (1995)

God has created us so that the heart is supposed to follow the head.

Chosen by God (1986)

He is indeed a God who sees. He sees everything that takes place in the universe. It is in full view of His eyes.

If there is anything about the character of God that repels people from Him more than His holiness, it is His omniscience.

Does God Control Everything? (2012)

Spiritually speaking, the pain of guilt can signal to us that something is wrong with our souls. There is a remedy for that and it's the same one that the church has always offered, namely, forgiveness. Real guilt requires real forgiveness.

The Christian is always a target for criticisms that may or may not be valid.

How Can I Develop a Christian Conscience? (2013)

It is exceedingly important that Christians know who the Holy Spirit is and understand something of the vital role He plays in their lives.

God's being is not dependent on anything or derived from anything. He has the power to be in and of Himself.

Who Is the Holy Spirit? (2012)

If we can read the newspaper or blogs, we can read the Bible. In fact, I venture to guess that more difficult words and concepts are expressed on the front page of a newspaper than on most pages of the Bible.

Bible characters are full of life. There is a unique quality of passion about them. Their lives reveal drama, pathos, lust, crime, devotion, and every conceivable aspect of human existence.

Knowing Scripture (2009)

The Christian bothers to engage in apologetics because, quite simply, how will the nonbeliever hear the truth of Christ Jesus "without someone preaching" (Romans 10:14)?

Apologetics. . .is not merely about winning an argument. It is about winning souls.

Defending Your Faith (2003)

Psychiatrists will never understand the human psyche to the degree the Creator understands that which He made. God knows our frame; it is He who made us so fearfully and wonderfully. All the nuances and complexities that bombard our senses and coalesce to produce a human personality are known in their intimate details by the divine mind.

The proof of our love is obedience to Christ's commands.

How Should I Live in This World? (2009)

SPURGEON, CHARLES HADDON

Caught in a snowstorm, a sixteen-year-old boy took refuge in a Methodist chapel. Inside he heard the words declared, "Look unto me, and be ye saved, all the ends of the earth, for I am God, and there is none else." From that moment his life was changed. Four years later he was pastor of the largest Baptist congregation in London. Charles Haddon Spurgeon was on his way to becoming one of the most influential preachers of the nineteenth century.

Seven years later his church moved to the newly built Metropolitan Chapel. With space for six thousand worshippers, the Metropolitan was the "megachurch" of its day.

A Baptist who was sometimes at odds with the Baptist Church, Spurgeon's appeal crossed many denominational boundaries.

He was born in 1834 and died in France in 1892.

His books include *A Good Start*, *The Greatest Fight in the World*, and *The Wordless Book*.

✍

The Lord's mercy often rides to the door of our hearts on the black horse of affliction.

There is no place like Calvary for creating confidence. The air of that sacred hill brings health to trembling faith.

He casts our sins behind His back, He blots them out; He says that though they be sought for, they shall not be found.

Be thankful for the providence which has made you poor, or sick, or sad; for by all this Jesus works the life of your spirit and turns you to Himself.

He that has long been on the road to Heaven finds that there was good reason why it was promised that his shoes should be iron and brass, for the road is rough. It will amaze the universe to see us enter the pearly gate, blameless in the day of our Lord Jesus Christ.

The Holy Spirit can cast out the evil spirit of the fear of man. He can make the coward brave.

Is it not most hopeful for men that a Man is now on the throne of the universe?

Our Lord Jesus did not die for imaginary sins, but His heart's blood was spilt to wash out deep crimson stains, which nothing else can remove.

It is well for us that as sin lives, and the flesh lives, and the devil lives, so Jesus lives; and it is also well that whatever might these may have to ruin us, Jesus has still greater power to save us.

I venture to say that a sinner justified by God stands on even a surer footing than a righteous man justified by his works, if such there be.

No tongue can tell the depth of that calm which comes over the soul which has received the peace of God which passeth all understanding.

What is it to bring the man out of his sepulchre if you leave him dead? Why lead him into the light if he is still blind? We thank God, that He who forgives our iniquities also heals our diseases.

You can never be poor while Jesus is rich, since you are in one firm with Him. Want can never assail you, since you are joint-proprietor with Him who is Possessor of Heaven and earth.

Repentance and forgiveness are riveted together by the eternal purpose of God. What God hath joined together let no man put asunder.

Do not make any mistake about it; repentance is not a thing of days and weeks, a temporary penance to be over as fast as possible! No; it is the grace of a lifetime, like faith itself.

Let us join hands and stand together at the foot of the cross, and trust our souls once for all to Him who shed His blood for the guilty. We will be saved by one and the same Savior.

He did not come to save us because we were worth the saving, but because we were utterly worthless, ruined, and undone.

Faith occupies the position of a channel or conduit pipe. Grace is the fountain and the stream; faith is the aqueduct along which the flood of mercy flows down to refresh the thirsty sons of men.

Love to God is obedience, love to God is holiness. To love God and to love man is to be conformed to the image of Christ; and this is salvation.

Great messages can be sent along slender wires, and the peace-giving witness of the Holy Spirit can reach the heart by means of a thread-like faith which seems almost unable to sustain its own weight.

What is faith? It is made up of three things—knowledge, belief, and trust.

You cannot turn anywhere in life without seeing faith in operation between man and man, or between man and natural law.

I would be glad to talk all night to bona fide sinners. The inn of mercy never closes its doors upon such, neither weekdays nor Sunday.

"Oh," said the devil to Martin Luther, "you are a sinner." "Yes," said he, "Christ died to save sinners." Thus he smote him with his own sword.

Recollect the question which flashed into the mind of young Bunyan when at his sports on the green on Sunday: "Wilt thou have thy sins and go to hell, or wilt thou quit thy sins and go to heaven?" That brought him to a dead stand.

The doctrine of the cross can be used to slay sin, even as the old warriors used their huge two-handed swords, and mowed down their foes at every stroke.

He who may have a treasure simply by his grasping it will be foolish indeed if he remains poor.

The world is no friend to grace. The best we can do with this world is to get through it as quickly as we can, for we dwell in an enemy's country.

All of Grace (c. 1880)

What is heaven, but to be with God, to dwell with Him, to realize that God is mine, and I am His?

He has made Christ heir of all things, and He has made you joint-heir with Him; and hence He has given you everything.

The new covenant is not founded on works at all, it is a covenant of pure unmingled grace.

What is gold compared with thy God? Thou couldst not live on it; thy spiritual life could not be sustained by it. Apply it to thy aching head, and would it afford thee any ease?

It is not often that God's people get the riches of this world, and that does but prove that riches are little worth, else God would give them to us.

Let vile persons and vile ways be contemned in your eyes: be of more noble spirits than to be companions with them. Regard not their societies, nor their scorns; their flatteries or their frowns.

"God in the Covenant" sermon (1856)

The child of God knows his good works do not make him acceptable to God, for he was acceptable to God by Jesus Christ long before he had any good works.

Say not "Our Father," and then look upon thy brethren with a sneer or a frown. I beseech thee, live like a brother, and act like a brother.

Talk of princes, and kings, and potentates: Their inheritance is but a pitiful foot of land, across which the bird's wing can soon direct its flight; but the broad acres of the Christian cannot be measured by eternity. He is rich, without a limit to his wealth. He is blessed, without a boundary to his bliss.

I must pour out my heart in the language which his Spirit gives me; and more than that, I must trust in the Spirit to speak the unutterable groanings of my spirit, when my lips cannot actually express all the emotions of my heart.

Save heaven itself there is nought more blissful than to enjoy that spirit of adoption.

"The Fatherhood of God" sermon (1858)

The law is a rough thing; Mount Sinai is a rough thing. Woe unto the watchman that warns not the ungodly!

We love to speak about the sweet promises of God; but if we could ever suppose that one of them could be changed, we would not talk anything more about them.

The highest science, the loftiest speculation, the mightiest philosophy, which can ever engage the attention of a child of God, is the name, the nature, the person, the work, the doings, and the existence of the great God whom he calls his Father.

God is perpetually the same. He is not composed of any substance or material, but is spirit—pure, essential, and ethereal spirit—and therefore He is immutable.

You do not understand what trouble means; you have hardly sipped the cup of trouble; you have only had a drop or two, but Jesus drank the dregs.

"The Immutability of God" sermon (1855)

Nobody would think of mutilating Milton's poems so, taking a few lines out of *Paradise Lost*, and then imagining that he could really get at the heart of the poet's power. So, always look at texts in the connection in which they stand.

Before the first star was kindled, before the first living creature began to sing the praise of its Creator, he loved his Church with an everlasting love.

"The Unchangeable Christ" sermon (1888)

Mighty minds are from time to time discovered in men whose limbs are wearing the chains of slavery, and whose backs are laid bare to the whip—they have black skins, but are in mind vastly superior to their brutal masters.

Grace is something not which I improve, but which improves me, employs me, works on me.

O thou who art gifted with a noble frame, a comely body, boast not thyself therein, for thy gifts come from God.

There are two boys, educated it may be in the same school, by the same master, and they shall apply themselves to their studies with the same diligence, but yet one shall far outstrip his fellow. Why is this? Because God hath asserted His sovereignty over the intellect as well as the body.

I dare not say, "Our Father which art in heaven," till I am regenerated. I cannot rejoice in the fatherhood of God towards me till I know that I am one with Him, and a joint heir with Christ.

"Divine Sovereignty" sermon (1856)

If you have ever come to God, crying out for salvation, and for salvation only, then you have come unto God aright.

"Salvation to the Uttermost" sermon (1856)

Those who hold God's Word, never need add something untrue in speaking to men. The sturdy truth of God touches every chord in every man's heart.

"The Holy Ghost—the Great Teacher" sermon (1855)

Since the world was created, man has imitated Satan; the creature of a day, the ephemera of an hour, has sought to match itself with the Eternal.

A sense of sin is all we have to look for as ministers. We preach to sinners; and let us know that a man will take the title of sinner to himself, and we then say to him, "Look unto Christ, and ye shall be saved."

When kings die, and in funeral pomp are carried to the grave, we are taught the lesson—"I am God, and beside Me there is none else."

"Sovereignty and Salvation" sermon (1856)

Gentlemen, pull the velvet out of your mouths; speak God's Word.

Blessed Bible! thou art all truth.

"The Bible" sermon (1855)

Men do not write well unless they have some end in writing. To sit down with paper and ink before you, and so much space to fill up, will ensure very poor writing.

Hold fast to eternal salvation through the eternal covenant carried out by eternal love unto eternal life.

"The Blessing of Full Assurance" sermon (1888)

Jesus comes to little ones.

If we be like trees planted by the rivers of water, bringing forth our fruit in our season, it is not because we were naturally fruitful, but because of the rivers of water by which we were planted. It is Jesus that makes us fruitful.

"The Incarnation and Birth of Christ" sermon (1855)

Do what you may, strive as earnestly as you can, live as excellently as you please, make what sacrifices you choose, be as eminent as you can for everything that is lovely and of good repute, yet none of these things can be pleasing to God unless they be mixed with faith.

A man who has not faith proves that he cannot stoop; for he has not faith for this reason, because he is too proud to believe. He declares he will not yield his intellect, he will not become a child and believe meekly what God tells him to believe.

"Faith" sermon (1856)

God knows where every particle of the handful of dust has gone: he has marked in his book the wandering of every one of its atoms. He hath death so open before His view, that He can bring all these together, bone to bone, and clothe them with the very flesh that robed them in the days of yore, and make them live again.

I beseech you, do not add to your eternal misery being a wolf in sheep's clothing. Show the cloven foot; do not hide it.

O brethren, above all things shun hypocrisy. If ye mean to be damned, make up your minds to it, and be damned like honest men; but do not, I beseech you, pretend to go to heaven while all the time you are going to hell.

"God, the All-Seeing One" sermon (1858)

Scrupulous truthfulness should always characterize everyone who stands up to proclaim the truth of God.

I met another man who considered himself perfect, but he was thoroughly mad; and I do not believe that any of the pretenders to perfection are better than good maniacs. . .for, while a man has got a spark of reason left in him, he cannot, unless he is the most impudent of impostors, talk about being perfect.

C. H. Spurgeon's Autobiography (1897)

Hope sees a crown in reserve, mansions in readiness, and Jesus Himself preparing a place for us, and by the rapturous sight she sustains the soul under the sorrows of the hour.

"The Holy Spirit's Intercession" sermon (1880)

If Abram, after years of holy living, is not justified by his works, but is accepted before God on account of his faith, much more must this be the case with the ungodly sinner who, having lived in unrighteousness, yet believeth on Jesus and is saved.

"Justification by Faith—Illustrated by Abram's Righteousness" sermon (1868)

A steadfast gaze into heaven may be to a devout soul a high order of worship, but if this filled up much of our working time it might become the idlest form of folly.

"The Ascension and the Second Advent Practically Considered" sermon (1884)

He saw thee ruined in the fall of thy father Adam, but His mind never changed from His purpose to save thee.

Who shall counsel the Most High to cast off the darlings of His bosom, or persuade the Savior to reject His spouse?

"The Infallibility of God's Purpose" sermon (1861)

We think that we do well to be angry with the rebellious, and so we prove ourselves to be more like Jonah than Jesus.

Not yet the thunderbolt! Not yet the riven heavens and the reeling earth! Not yet the great white throne, and the day of judgment; for he is very pitiful, and beareth long with men!

"God's Longsuffering" sermon (1886)

If you want to praise the Lord Jesus Christ, tell the people about Him. Take of the things of Christ, and show them to the people, and you will glorify Christ.

There is no salvation apart from the Trinity. It must be the Father, the Son, and the Holy Ghost.

The darker the night grows, and the fiercer the storm becomes, the better will we remember that He of the lake of Galilee came to them upon the waves in the night when the storm was wildest.

"Honey in the Mouth!" sermon (1891)

It is an honor to believe what the lips of Jesus taught. I had sooner be a fool with Christ than a wise man with the philosophers.

"Christ Precious to Believers" sermon (1890)

Is there anything more powerful than the sword of the Spirit? That has not pierced the man's heart; is there anything else which will do it?

The Christian life was intended not to be a sitting still, but a race, a perpetual motion.

"Final Perseverance" sermon (1856)

The wicked man, when he dies, is driven to his grave, but the Christian comes to his grave.

We do not believe all that Job's friends said.

"The Death of the Christian" sermon (1855)

Sanctification grows out of faith in Jesus Christ. Remember holiness is a flower, not a root; it is not sanctification that saves, but salvation that sanctifies.

Men of God, if you are indeed the Lord's, and feel that you are His, begin now to intercede for all who belong to you. Never be satisfied unless they are saved too.

"Consecration to God" sermon (1868)

Walking by sight is just this: "I believe in myself." Whereas walking by faith is: "I believe in God."

We must wear our piety, not as some holiday garment, but as our everyday dress.

"Faith versus Sight" sermon (1866)

When man fell in the garden, manhood fell entirely; there was not one single pillar in the temple of manhood that stood erect.

"Human Inability" sermon (1858)

God has forgiven us continuously. He not only forgave us at the first all our sins, but He continues daily to forgive, for the act of forgiveness is a continuous one.

"Forgiveness Made Easy" sermon (1878)

Godliness is a lifelong business. The working out of the salvation that the Lord, Himself, works in you is not a matter of certain hours, or of a limited period of life. Salvation is unfolded throughout our entire sojourn here.

"The Watchword for Today—'Stand Fast,'" sermon (1887)

Prayer is the never-failing resort of the Christian in any case and in every plight.

"The Believer Sinking in the Mire" sermon (1865)

Tomorrow—it is not written in the almanac of time. Tomorrow—it is in Satan's calendar, and nowhere else. . . . Yonder clock saith "today"; everything crieth "today."

"Effectual Calling" sermon (1856)

God's people have always in their worst condition found out the best of their God.

They who dive in the sea of affliction, bring up rare pearls.

Prevailing prayer is victorious over the God of mercy.

We know not how much capacity for usefulness there may be in us.

You cannot guess how greatly God will bless you. Only go and stand at His door, you cannot tell what is in reserve for you.

"The Golden Key of Prayer" sermon (1865)

True prayer is the trading of the heart with God, and the heart never comes into spiritual commerce with the ports of heaven until God the Holy Ghost puts wind into the sails and speeds the ship into its haven.

If you rest on the finished work of Jesus you have already the best evidence of your salvation in the world; you have God's word for it; what more is needed?

"The Raven's Cry" sermon (1866)

STANLEY, ANDY

Andy Stanley was born in Atlanta, Georgia, in 1958. In college he was study-ing journalism when a position as youth minister opened up in his father's church. He took the position at the First Baptist Church of Atlanta. Five years afterward he and his colleagues founded the North Point Community Church. It began with the premise that Atlanta didn't need another church. It needed a place where the unchurched could hear that Jesus loved them and died for their sins.

North Point Community Church grew into North Point Ministries. The church and the pastor, Andy Stanley, are regularly listed as being among the most influential in the United States.

His books include *Deep and Wide*, *Next Generation Leader*, *Seven Practices of Effective Ministry*, and *The Grace of God*.

✍

Rebellion never goes without consequences.

Sex is not for mature people. Sex is not for ready people. Sex is not for in-love people. Sex is for married people.

The Seven Checkpoints (2001)

We hurt most who we love the most. Bad grammar, painful truth.

As long as you are carrying a secret, as long as you are trying to ease your conscience by telling God how sorry you are, you are setting yourself up to repeat the past.

It Came from Within! (2001)

There in the midst of unjust treatment and seemingly undeserved pain, the true character of a man or woman is revealed. Pretense is peeled away.

Your character is who you really are.

Louder Than Words (2004)

No one gets to the place where he no longer needs wise counsel. Nobody.

God's will for your life will always line up with His law, His principles, and His wisdom.

The Principle of the Path (2008)

The leader who refuses to move until the fear is gone will never move. Consequently, he will never lead.

Acknowledging weakness doesn't make a leader less effective. On the contrary, in most cases it is simply a way of expressing that he understands what everyone else has known for some time. When you acknowledge your weaknesses to the rest of your team, it is never new information.

The Next Generation Leader (2003)

The God of Christianity never claims to be fair. He goes beyond fair. The Bible teaches that He decided not to give us what we deserve—that's mercy. In addition, God decided to give us exactly what we didn't deserve—we call that grace.

Is Christianity fair? It is certainly not fair to God. Christians believe that God sent His Son to die for your sins and mine. Fairness would demand that we die for our own sins.

How Good Is Good Enough? (2003)

Sowing in faith results in an eternal crop. Cowering in fear yields empty fields.

A farmer doesn't acquire seed to consume it or hoard it. He only decides where to plant it. And only when the seed has been irrevocably cast into the ground is a harvest returned.

Fields of Gold (2004)

Here is a major announcement brought to you by the God of the universe: Lost people are going to act lost—because they are lost!

Will you be the one influenced by others—or the one who influences others for Christ?

Max Q Student Journal (with Stuart Hall, 2004)

STANLEY, CHARLES

Born in Dry Fork, Virginia, in 1932, Charles Stanley became a born-again Christian at the age of twelve and began preaching at the age of fourteen. He joined the First Baptist Church of Atlanta when he was thirty-seven and became senior pastor two years later, a post he has held for more than thirty years.

In 1982 he founded In Touch Ministries. His *In Touch with Dr. Charles Stanley* broadcasts, tackling such issues as finances, parenting, relationships, and Christianity, can now be heard on more than five hundred radio stations and three hundred television stations.

His books include *The Source of My Strength*, *The Charles F. Stanley Life Principles Book*, *In Step with God: Understanding His Ways and Plans for Your Life*, and *How to Reach Your Full Potential for God*.

☜

We must never limit God's ability to turn even the worst, most vile experience in our lives into something productive, beneficial and positive.

Regardless of the source of our pain, we must accept that God knows, God loves and God is at work.

The Blessings of Brokenness (1997)

The reason so many of us struggle so intensely with adversity is that we have yet to adopt God's perspective and priorities.

If you are a child of God whose heart's desire is to see God glorified through you, adversity will not put you down for the count. There will be those initial moments of shock and confusion. But the man or woman who has God's perspective on this life and the life to come will always emerge victorious!

How to Handle Adversity (1989)

Focusing on difficulties intensifies and enlarges the problem. When we focus our attention on God, the problem is put into its proper perspective and it no longer overwhelms us.

If we walk in the Spirit daily, surrendered to His power, we have the right to expect anything we need to hear from God. The Holy Spirit living within us and speaking to us ought to be the natural, normal lifestyle of believers.

How to Listen to God (2002)

What really matters is not what we think we perceive, or what others tell us is the truth, but what God says is the accurate perception and the truth of any situation.

The lies of the devil always have a ring of truth to them. The best counterfeit is always as close to the original as possible.

When the Enemy Strikes (2004)

The awful, never-ending process of combating temptation is God's means of maturing us and conforming us to the image of Christ.

God has set a limit on the intensity of every temptation. God knows you perfectly, inside and out. In accordance with His perfect knowledge He has set a limit on the intensity of the temptations you will face.

Winning the War Within (1998)

The fruit of the Spirit was never intended to be a demonstration of our dedication and resolve. It is the evidence of our dependency on and sensitivity to the promptings of the Spirit.

The Holy Spirit's power cannot be harnessed. His power cannot be used to accomplish anything other than the Father's will. He is not a candy dispenser. He is not a vending machine. He is not a genie waiting for someone to rub His lamp the right way. He is holy God.

The Wonderful Spirit-Filled Life (1992)

Remember, the shortest distance between a problem and the solution is the distance between our knees and the floor.

God wants us to seek Him more than anything else, even more than we seek answers to prayer. When we come to God in prayer, sometimes our hearts are so full of what we want that we leave God out. Our minds become consumed with the gift rather than the giver.

Handle with Prayer (1987)

The dark moments of our life will last only as long as is necessary for God to accomplish His purpose in us.

Brokenness is God's requirement for maximum usefulness.

30 Life Principles Study Guide (2008)

STOTT, JOHN

John Robert Walmsley Stott, born to a leading London doctor in 1921, was at boarding school when he heard a sermon on Revelation 3:20: "Behold, I stand at the door, and knock: if any man hear my voice, and open the door, I will come in to him, and will sup with him, and he with me."

Realizing he had been holding Jesus at arm's length, he decided to let Him in—and that made all the difference in his life. Later he became rector at the same church (All Souls in London) he had attended as a boy.

He became well known on the national and international church scene. In 1974 he founded John Stott Ministries, and in 1982 the London Institute for Contemporary Christianity, of which he remained honorary president until his death.

After his death in 2011, *Christianity Today* called him "an architect of twentieth-century evangelicalism who shaped the faith of a generation."

His written works include *Basic Christianity*, *The Cross of Christ*, and *Essentials*.

A deaf church is a dead church: that is an unalterable principle.

Behind the concept and the act of preaching there lies a doctrine of God, a conviction about His being, His action, and His purpose. The kind of God we believe in determines the kind of sermons we preach.

Between Two Worlds: The Challenge of Preaching Today (1982)

Envy is the reverse side of a coin called vanity. Nobody is ever envious of others who is not first proud of himself.

The Lord's Supper that Jesus instituted was not meant to be a slightly sentimental forget-me-not, but rather a service rich in spiritual significance.

The Cross of Christ (1986)

There is an urgent need in the church today for more genuinely Christian thinkers, who have not capitulated to the prevailing secularism, that is to say, for more Christians who have put their minds under the yoke of Christ.

Jesus came not only to teach but to save, not only to reveal God to human beings, but also to redeem human beings for God. This is because our major problem is not our ignorance but our sin and guilt.

Life in Christ (2003)

Before we decided to look for God, God had already been looking for us.

In seeking God we have to be prepared, not only to revise our ideas but to reform our lives.

Basic Christianity (1958)

Do not be content with a static Christian life. Determine rather to grow in faith and love, in knowledge and holiness.

When Jesus is truly our Lord, He directs our lives and we gladly obey Him. Indeed, we bring every part of our lives under His lordship—our home and family, our sexuality and marriage, our job or unemployment, our money and possessions, our ambitions and recreations.

Christian Basics (1991)

STOWELL, JOSEPH

Dr. Joseph M. Stowell III, born in 1944, has served as president of the Moody Bible Institute, teaching pastor at Harvest Bible Chapel, and a board member of the Billy Graham Evangelical Association. Currently he serves as president of Cornerstone University.

He sees his work at Cornerstone as developing "people who can go into our world and bring the redemptive and transforming values of Christ's kingdom into the culture in which they find themselves."

His Internet ministry, Strength for the Journey, features daily and weekly messages, downloadable Bible study materials, and an audio library of his sermons.

He has written over twenty books, including *Why It's Hard to Love Jesus*, *Radical Reliance: Living 24/7 with God at the Center*, *Living the Life God Has Planned*, and *Strength for the Journey*.

✍

Authentic Christianity is not just about keeping and protecting the faith and keeping the rules. It is even more than living to deepen your relationship with Jesus. Authentic Christianity, the real deal, is about embracing all of these important elements.

The basic human need to be accepted and affirmed has not changed. Jesus offers to satisfy this longing. He is looking to extend the gracious offer through followers who practice the happy art of sharing in an unusual and enriching love for one another regardless.

The Trouble with Jesus (2003)

A true Christian experience has its source in and is motivated by a personal relationship with Christ. Not just a personal relationship that saves me, but a relationship that determines my behavior, responses, thoughts, and actions in ways that would be particularly pleasing to Him.

Christ is concerned with more than what we do. He is initially concerned about why we do what we do. Christ wants our external activities to be produced out of a personal relationship with Him. He demands something deeper than habit, more significant than ritual, more delightful than duty for duty's sake.

Fan the Flame (1983)

If Christianity is dull and boring, if it is a burden and not a blessing, then most likely we are involved in a project, not a Person—a system not a Savior, rules rather than a relationship.

Perhaps the greatest self-deceit is to tell ourselves that we can be self-sufficient.

Following Christ (1996)

All of creation was created to glorify God. God intended that we would join the created world in reflecting the beauty and strength of His magnificent character. Pain and trouble are the graffiti that Satan scrawls across the face of God's glory.

God is able to transform us. He knows what is best. He knows what it takes. He will, as the loving, all-powerful sculptor, chip away until Jesus is seen in the hardened hunk of our lives.

Through the Fire (1985)

Until we see God in His terrifying size and limitless scope, we will never see ourselves as we really are. Nor will we fully appreciate the fact that He chose to love you and me.

Seeking the approval of others always leads us away from what matters. Jesus wants my heart. He's most concerned about my relationship to Him.

Why It's Hard to Love Jesus (2003)

Division among God's people gives Satan a tremendous advantage in conquering our usefulness, joy, and peace. The destructive influence of murmuring, contentious words must be exchanged for words that produce confidence in Christ and encouragement to His people.

Divine love is not an emotional response, but an act of the will. Divine love is expressed not necessarily because we "feel" like it, but because we choose to love. If we wait to "feel" like loving someone, our love will be erratic and arbitrary.

Tongue in Check (1983)

SUNDAY, BILLY

Born in Ames, Iowa, in 1862, William Ashley Sunday began his career in the public eye as a baseball player with the Chicago White Stockings. He went on to play with the Pittsburgh Alleghenys and the Philadelphia Phillies.

After coming to faith he turned down a lucrative baseball contract for a low-paid position working and preaching at the YMCA. Three years later he met evangelist J. Wilbur Chapman. Inspired by the man, Sunday began to work with him. When Chapman retired from evangelizing, Sunday filled his place, going out on the road and attracting steadily larger crowds.

A Presbyterian himself (he once said he was Presbyterian because the woman he loved was), his ministry was nondenominational. He died in 1935 in Chicago, Illinois. His life inspired many biographies.

✍

Show me the nation that has ever crumbled into oblivion and decay that was governed by Christian beliefs.

What has Jesus Christ ever asked you to do that wasn't for your own good?

The Best of Billy Sunday (1965)

There never was a doubt in the world that didn't come straight from the devil.

You never hear of a man marrying a woman to reform her.

Don't throw any mud at the plan of salvation until you try it and find out that it won't work.

Temptation is not sin. Yielding is.

The Real Billy Sunday (1914)

More people fail from lack of purpose than from lack of talent.

A mother's love is unselfish and has no limits this side of heaven.

I do not believe there are devils enough to pull a boy or girl out of the arms of a Christian mother.

If fate clips your wings and casts you on the humbler plains of life, be a hero there.

Though sowing wild oats may have a kick in it, it is the harvest that brings the curse to the sowers and tears of sorrow to the father and mother.

The Sawdust Trail (1932)

SWINDOLL, CHARLES

Born in 1924 in El Campo, Texas, Charles (Chuck) Swindoll felt the call to ministry while on military service in Okinawa. After completing his time with the Marine Corps, he enrolled in Dallas Theological Seminary. After a pastoral career that took in many churches, he founded the Stonebriar Community Church in Frisco, Texas, where he is senior pastor-teacher.

His regular broadcast, *Insight for Living*, has aired on Christian radio stations around the world since 1979.

In 2009 a survey of Protestant pastors placed Charles Swindoll second only to Billy Graham in a list of preachers who had influenced them the most.

His books include *The Church Awakening*, *The Owner's Manual for Christians*, *So You Want to be Like Christ: Eight Essentials to Get You There*, and *Behold—The Man!*

Allowing anger to seethe on the back burner will lead to a very large lid blowing off a very hot pot.

No one is immune to temptation. Not even a hero. Not even a nobody. Not even people like you and me. Lust is never very far away. And just when you least expect it, there it is again.

Man to Man (1996)

God did not give us His Word to satisfy our curiosity, but to change our lives.
"Our Library of Living Truth" sermon (1978)

God's desire is that there be a conscious, consistent transfer of God's truth from the older to the younger in the family.

What is true of a nation and what is true of people in the Bible is also true of families.

Growing Wise in Family Life (1988)

Jesus could not pay the price for our sin by hiding in the safety of the upper room, and we cannot remain in the safety of the sanctuary.

Having accepted the Father's will over our own, we are then ready to face our own Calvary.

The Darkness and the Dawn (2001)

David lived by a very simple principle. Nothing to prove and nothing to lose.

No matter how big the giant might be in anyone's life—God is greater than that giant.

We remember what we ought to forget and forget what we ought to remember.

Fear takes one giant and turns it into a whole population.

"David and the Dwarf" sermon (2009)

My determination is to transfer this habit of worry into an instant moment of prayer and leave it with God.

"Prayer: Calling Out" sermon (2004)

Death may be the final destination in our earthly journey, but it is merely the tunnel that transports us to the very real world beyond.

Hell is as real to those who die without Christ as heaven is to the child of God.

There will be no second chance after death. The time to prepare is now.

"Visiting the Real Twilight Zone" sermon (1985)

Lead with actions and let the feelings follow.

Insight for Living broadcast (2009)

I don't think anything concerns me more than using grace as a tool to justify sin.

Grace means that in forgiving you, God gives you the strength to endure the consequences. It does not mean the consequences are automatically removed.

"Trouble at Home" sermon (2009)

If you want to stop an argument, close your mouth.

If you never get criticized, chances are you aren't getting anything done.

Hand Me Another Brick (1981)

Our Lord wants His true followers to be distinct, unlike the majority who follow the herd. In solving conflicts, doing business, and responding to difficulties, Jesus' people are not to maintain the same attitudes or choose the priorities of the majority.

Only people who keep short accounts of their own failures, sins, and weaknesses have earned the right to assist others with those things in their lives. Vulnerable, humble, transparent individuals make the best confronters.

Simple Faith (1991)

Our inner "self" doesn't want to dump God entirely, just keep Him at a comfortable distance.

The "celebrity syndrome" so present in our Christian thought and activities just doesn't square with the attitudes and messages of Jesus.

Improving Your Serve (1981)

An attitude that releases joy begins with your knowing Christ in a personal way and allowing Him to take the blows of life for you.
I know of no greater need today than the need for joy. Unexplainable, contagious joy. Outrageous joy.

Laugh Again (1995)

Interestingly, the Bible says little about success, but a lot about the heart, the place where true success originates.

Successes can easily become failures. All it takes is letting our guard down.

The Quest for Character (1982)

Focusing intently on Christ naturally results in a lifestyle of greater and greater selflessness.

A "godly" person is one who ceases to be self-centered in order to become God-centered.

So You Want to Be Like Christ? (2005)

TADA, JONI EARECKSON

Born in Baltimore, Maryland, in 1949, Joni Eareckson was an active teenager until a diving accident in Chesapeake Bay broke her neck and left her a quadriplegic. The period that followed was a dark one, but her faith and two years of rehabilitation and art therapy (during which she learned to paint with a brush held between her teeth) brought her through it. The story of those years became an international bestseller and was turned into a movie.

In 1979 she founded Joni and Friends, a worldwide Christian ministry for people with disabilities. She married in 1982 and, in 2006, the Joni and Friends International Disability Center was established in Agoura Hills, California.

She has been inducted into the Christian Booksellers' Association's Hall of Honor.

Her books include *Joni*, *A Step Further*, *Friendship Unlimited: How You Can Help a Disabled Friend*, and *Finding God in Hidden Places*.

✍

Great faith believes in God even when He plays His hand close to His vest, never showing all His cards. He has His reasons for doing so. God wants to increase your "measure of faith." He does this whenever He conceals a matter, and you trust Him nevertheless!

Physical pain can cloud our convictions about God's benefits, which is why I must continually stir my soul to remember them.

Pearls of Great Price (2006)

Even though pain and suffering may be our experience during our brief earthly passage, our Lord knows how to turn even such disappointments and hardships toward our favor and help.

One of the reasons I *know* the Bible is true is by the way its wisdom runs consistently cross-grain to common human assumptions. God's Word never, ever tags along behind human thinking and philosophies, never tries to stay in style, never seeks to accommodate itself or somehow make itself "relevant."

A Place of Healing (2010)

When the Bible talks about waiting, it means *confidently trusting* that God knows how much suffering I need and can take. It means *looking expectantly* toward the time when He will free me from my burdens.

How did Jesus deal with sin? He dealt with it by paying its penalty on the cross and by confronting sinful actions and attitudes in people He met.

A Step Further (1978)

We pilgrims walk the tightrope between earth and heaven, feeling trapped in time, yet with eternity beating in our hearts. Our unsatisfied sense of exile is not to be solved or fixed while here on earth.

Let your imagination run wild for a moment. Jesus has gone on to prepare a place for us, and each of us is to have a big mansion—no down payment or mortgage to worry about, thankfully—on a golden avenue overlooking fields and flowers. Wow!

Heaven (1995)

Although it's true the Lord will never do exactly the same thing a second time around, He will do something better. A new thing. A new way. God specializes in things fresh and firsthand.

He is not satisfied with the updated and revised version—He's always quick to create something new.

God can exchange the tragic meaning behind accidents or injuries for something new and positive.

Diamonds in the Dust (1993)

The Bible reveals God's soul to us in a way no other book is able to do.

More Precious Than Silver (1998)

When you are in so much pain, sorrow, or frustration that it feels as though your heart might burst within you, when you feel like your soul has been torn like rotten fabric, God draws close to help. You don't even have to dial 911 or push that little blue On-Star button. He's there with you instantly, ready to hear and respond to your cries of perplexity and anguish.

The fact is, gut-wrenching questions honor God. Despair directed at His throne is a way of encountering Him, opening ourselves up to the one and only Someone who can actually do something about our plight.

A Lifetime of Wisdom (2009)

TCHIVIDJIAN, GIGI GRAHAM

Born in Montreat, North Carolina, in 1945, Gigi (Virginia) is the eldest daughter of evangelist Billy Graham. She has lived in Switzerland, Israel, Wisconsin, and Florida.

Initially overawed by her father's reputation and afraid she might not live up to it, Gigi found peace in the realization that God had a different plan for her. She would be a wife, mother, and grandmother, sharing rather than evangelizing and finding God in the small things.

She is a popular speaker at conferences and rallies and has appeared on television several times. Her books and talks tend to focus on issues relating to women and the family in modern society.

Her books include *Thank You, Lord, for My Home*; *Currents of the Heart*; *A Search for Serenity, Sincerely. . . Gigi*, and *Diapers and Dishes or Pinstripes and Pumps*.

✍

A fish is free as long as it stays in the water. If it suddenly declares that it wants its freedom to fly in the air like a bird, disaster occurs. A train is free as long as it stays on the track. However, if it demands freedom to take off down a major highway, the result is destruction and devastation. We too can only experience true freedom in its fullest if we remain within the framework of freedom. Often this requires accepting responsibility and practicing discipline.

Whether your gift is mighty or humble, whether you exercise it in the marketplace or at the podium, in the executive suite or in the schoolroom, in the office or at home, your main task or gift or ministry is to be a light in a dark world.

For Women Only (2001)

TEN BOOM, CORRIE

Born in Amsterdam, Holland, in 1892, Cornelia ten Boom was a Dutch watchmaker's daughter who lived at home with her parents and siblings. She also ran a church that catered to people with mental disabilities and helped raise foster children.

She was forty-two years old when the Nazis invaded Holland. Two years later a Jewish woman appeared at the door of the family house saying her husband had been arrested and she feared she would be next. The ten Booms took her in, as well as many others, at the risk of their own lives. They were eventually discovered and sent to concentration camps. Some of the family died there, but most of the people they hid survived.

Israel named her Righteous Among the Nations, and she traveled the world as a speaker until her death in California in 1983.

She told her story in the book *The Hiding Place*.

☝

Satan sometimes suggests that an offering will satisfy God, when in fact He is demanding our all.

The devil smiles when we are up to our ears in work, but he trembles when we pray.

Not Good If Detached (1957)

God promises us forgiveness for what we have done, but we need His deliverance from what we are.

I have experienced His presence in the deepest hell that man can create. I have really tested the promises of the Bible, and believe me, you can count on them.

He Cares, He Comforts (1977)

Every experience God gives us, every person He puts in our lives is the perfect preparation for the future that only He can see.

The Hiding Place (with John and Elizabeth Sherrill, 1971)

Children need the wisdom of their elders; the aging need the encouragement of a child's exuberance.

In My Father's House (1976)

Jesus loves sinners. He only loves sinners. He has never turned anyone away who came to Him for forgiveness, and He died on the cross for sinners, not for respectable people.

When you come to Him, He will deliver you from your sins. But you also have to confess them and bring them to Him.

I Stand at the Door and Knock (2008)

Let us keep in mind that God wants and expects us to be conquerors over the powers of darkness, not only for the sake of personal victory and for the liberation of other souls from the chains of Satan (though this is very important. . .) but for His glory, so that His triumph and victory over His enemies may be demonstrated!

We have a good safeguard and guide, the Bible, God's Word. Here we find not only the necessary information about Satan and demons, but also the weapons and armor that we need for this battle, so that, through Jesus Christ, we may be more than conquerors.

Defeated Enemies (2002)

Worry does not empty tomorrow of its sorrow, it empties today of its strength.

Forgiveness is the key that unlocks the door of resentment and the handcuffs of hatred. It is a power that breaks the chains of bitterness and the shackles of selfishness.

Clippings from My Notebook (1982)

He uses our problems for His miracles. This was my first lesson in learning to trust Him completely.

Tramp for the Lord (1975)

The tree on the mountain takes whatever the weather brings. If it has any choice at all, it is in putting down roots as deeply as possible.

Jesus is Victor. Calvary is the place of victory. Obedience is the pathway of victory, Bible study and prayer the preparation. Courage, faith, the spirit of victory—every temptation is a chance for victory, a signal to fly the flag of our Victor, a chance to make the tempter know anew that he is defeated.

Each New Day (1977)

The Lord never makes a mistake. One day, when we are in heaven, I'm sure we shall see the answers to the *whys*.

No pit is so deep that the Lord is not deeper still.

Jesus Is Victor (1985)

THOMAS À KEMPIS

Born in 1389 in what is now Germany, Thomas à Kempis was actually Thomas Haemerkken. The title "Kempis" indicated that his hometown was Kempen, where he was a church canon, or "canon regular."

A large part of his life was spent copying religious texts (in the days before mass printing was available), but he also wrote several books of his own about the religious life.

He died in 1471 in modern-day Holland.

His written works include *Prayers and Meditations on the Life of Christ, Meditations on the Incarnation of Christ, Soliloquy of the Soul, The Imitation of Christ,* and many biographies of holy men.

✍

Christ was willing to suffer and be despised, and darest thou complain of anything?

We must not trust every saying or suggestion, but warily and patiently ponder things according to the will of God.

Who hath a greater combat than he that laboreth to overcome himself?

I have often heard, that it is safer to hear and to take counsel, than to give it.

No man doth safely rule, be he that hath learned gladly to obey.

If God were our one and only desire we would not be so easily upset when our opinions do not find outside acceptance.

A wise lover values not so much the gift of the lover as the love of the giver.

All men desire peace, but very few desire those things that make for peace.

Jesus has now many lovers of the heavenly kingdom but few bearers of His cross.

God hath thus ordered it, that we may learn to bear one another's burdens; for no man is without fault, no man without his burden, no man sufficient of himself, no man wise enough of himself; but we ought to bear with one another, comfort one another, help, instruct, and admonish one another.

By two wings is man lifted above earthly things, even by simplicity and purity. Simplicity ought to be in the intention, purity in the affection.

Learned arguments do not make a man holy and righteous, whereas a good life makes him dear to God.

All that is in the world is vanity except to love God and serve Him only.

Nothing is sweeter than love, nothing stronger or higher or wider, nothing is more pleasant, nothing fuller, and nothing better in heaven or on earth, for love is born of God and cannot rest except in God, who is created above all things.

The Lord bestows His blessings there, where He finds the vessels empty.

Fight like a man. Habit is overcome by habit.

At the least, bear patiently, if thou canst not joyfully. And although thou be very unwilling to hear it, and feel indignation, yet check thyself, and suffer no unadvised word to come forth from thy lips, whereby the little ones may be offended. Soon the storm which hath been raised shall be stilled, and inward grief shall be sweetened by returning grace.

Be ofttimes mindful of the saying, The eye is not satisfied with seeing, nor the ear with hearing. Strive, therefore, to turn away thy heart from the love of the things that are seen, and to set it upon the things that are not seen. For they who follow after their own fleshly lusts, defile the conscience, and destroy the grace of God.

Look at our fathers in the old days, living masterpieces as they are and shining examples of true religion; and see how feeble our own achievement is, almost nothing. Heaven help us, what is our life in comparison with theirs? Holy people these, true friends of Christ, that could go hungry and thirsty in

God's service; cold and ill-clad, worn out with labors and vigils and fasting, with praying and meditating on holy things, with all the persecutions and insults they endured.

God often grants in a moment what He has long denied.

Hence we must support one another, console one another, mutually help, counsel, and advise, for the measure of every man's virtue is best revealed in time of adversity—adversity that does not weaken a man but rather shows what he is.

Let temporal things be in the use, eternal things in the desire.

If you wish to draw profit, read with humility, simplicity, and faith, and never with the design of gaining a reputation for learning.

He is not truly patient who will only suffer as far as seems right to him and from whom he pleases. The truly patient man considers not by whom he is tried, one above him, or by an equal, or by an inferior, whether by a good and holy man or by a perverse and unworthy man, but from every creature. He gratefully accepts all from the hand of God and counts it gain.

If men used as much care in uprooting vices and implanting virtues as they do in discussing problems, there would not be so much evil and scandal in the world, or such laxity in religious organizations. On the day of judgment, surely, we shall not be asked what we have read but what we have done; not how well we have spoken but how well we have lived. Tell me, where now are all the masters and teachers whom you knew so well in life and who were famous for their learning? Others have already taken their places and I know not whether they ever think of their predecessors. During life they seemed to be something; now they are seldom remembered.

It is not really a small thing when in small things we resist self.

The deepest and most profitable lesson is this, the true knowledge and contempt of ourselves.

It is much safer to be subject than it is to command. Many live in obedience more from necessity than from love. Such become discontented and dejected on the slightest pretext; they will never gain peace of mind unless they subject themselves wholeheartedly for the love of God.

A lowly knowledge of thyself is a surer way to God than the deep searching of a man's learnings. Not that learning is to be blamed, nor the taking account of anything that is good; but a good conscience and a holy life is better than all. And because many seek knowledge rather than good living, therefore they go astray, and bear little or no fruit.

Today man is, and tomorrow he will be seen no more. And being removed out of sight, quickly also he is out of mind. O the dullness and hardness of man's heart, which thinketh only of the present, and looketh not forward to the future. Thou oughtest in every deed and thought so to order thyself, as if thou wert to die this day.

The world promises things that are temporal and small, and it is served with great eagerness. I [Christ] promise things that are great and eternal, and the hearts of mortals are slow to stir.

Therefore, neither confide in nor depend upon a wind-shaken reed, for "all flesh is grass" and all its glory, like the flower of grass, will fade away. You will quickly be deceived if you look only to the outward appearance of men, and you will often be disappointed if you seek comfort and gain in them.

Rest from inordinate desire or knowledge, for therein is found much distraction and deceit.

O true and heavenly grace, without which our own merits are nothing, and our natural gifts of no account! Neither arts nor riches, beauty nor strength, genius nor eloquence have any value in Your eyes, Lord, unless allied to grace. For the gifts of nature are common to good men and bad alike, but grace or love are Your especial gift to those whom You choose, and those who are sealed with this are counted worthy of life everlasting.

Many things there are to know which profiteth little or nothing to the soul.

He who shunneth not small faults falleth little by little into greater.

Two things specially avail unto improvement in holiness, namely firmness to withdraw ourselves from the sin to which by nature we are most inclined, and earnest zeal for that good in which we are most lacking.

Do not let your peace depend on the words of men. Their thinking well or badly of you does not make you different from what you are. Where are true peace and glory? Are they not in Me? He who neither cares to please men nor fears to displease them will enjoy great peace, for all unrest and distraction of the senses arise out of disorderly love and vain fear.

My child, I am the Lord who gives strength in the day of trouble. Come to Me when all is not well with you. Your tardiness in turning to prayer is the greatest obstacle to heavenly consolation, for before you pray earnestly to Me you first seek many comforts and take pleasure in outward things. Thus, all things are of little profit to you until you realize that I am the One who saves those who trust in Me, and that outside of Me there is no worthwhile help, or any useful counsel or lasting remedy.

What I have given, I can take away and restore when it pleases Me. What I give remains Mine, and thus when I take it away I take nothing that is yours, for every good gift and every perfect gift is Mine.

For a little reward men make a long journey; for eternal life many will scarce lift a foot once from the ground. Mean reward is sought after; for a single piece of money sometimes there is shameful striving; for a thing which is vain and for a trifling promise, men shrink not from toiling day and night.

Remain tranquil and prepare to bear still greater trials. All is not lost even though you be troubled oftener or tempted more grievously. You are a man, not God. You are flesh, not an angel. How can you possibly expect to remain always in the same state of virtue when the angels in heaven and the first man in paradise failed to do so? I am He who rescues the afflicted and brings to My divinity those who know their own weakness.

Pardon me also, and deal mercifully with me, as often as I think of anything besides You in prayer. For I confess truly that I am accustomed to be very much distracted. Very often I am not where bodily I stand or sit; rather, I am where my thoughts carry me. Where my thoughts are, there am I; and frequently my thoughts are where my love is. That which naturally delights, or is by habit pleasing, comes to me quickly. Hence You who are Truth itself, have plainly said: "For where your treasure is, there is your heart also." If I love heaven, I think willingly of heavenly things. If I love the world, I rejoice at the happiness of the world and grieve at its troubles. If I love the flesh, I often imagine things that are carnal. If I love the spirit, I delight in thinking of spiritual matters. For whatever I love, I am willing to speak and hear about.

Thou knowest well how to excuse and color thine own deeds, but thou art not willing to receive the excuses of others.

Occasions do not make a man frail, but they show what he is.

The Imitation of Christ (15th century)

In the Cross is salvation; in the Cross is life; in the Cross is protection against our enemies; in the Cross is infusion of heavenly sweetness; in the Cross is strength of mind; in the Cross is joy of spirit; in the Cross is excellence of virtue; in the Cross is perfection of holiness. There is no salvation of soul, nor hope of eternal life, save in the Cross.

The more humble and obedient to God a man is, the more wise and at peace he will be in all that he does.

Love flies, runs, leaps for joy; it is free and unrestrained. Love gives all for all, resting in One who is highest above all things, from whom every good flows and proceeds. Love does not regard the gifts, but turns to the Giver of all good gifts. Love knows no limits, but ardently transcends all bounds. Love feels no burden, takes no account of toil, attempts things beyond its strength; love sees nothing as impossible, for it feels able to achieve all things. Love therefore does great things; it is strange and effective; while he who lacks love faints and fails.

A sure way of retaining the grace of heaven is to disregard outward appearances, and diligently to cultivate such things as foster amendment of life and fervor of soul, rather than to cultivate those qualities that seem most popular.

If you desire to know or learn anything to your advantage, then take delight in being unknown and unregarded. A true understanding and humble estimate of oneself is the highest and most valuable of all lessons. To take no account of oneself, but always to think well and highly of others is the highest wisdom and perfection.

Let all your thoughts be with the Most High, and direct your humble prayers unceasingly to Christ. If you cannot contemplate high and heavenly things, take refuge in the Passion of Christ, and love to dwell within His Sacred Wounds. For if you devoutly seek the Wounds of Jesus and the precious marks of His Passion, you will find great strength in all troubles.

The Inner Life (15th century)

TORREY, R. A.

Reuben Archer Torrey was a Congregational minister who joined D. L. Moody in his evangelical work in 1889. He went on to become superintendent of what would become the Moody Bible Institute and pastor of the church in Chicago that would become the Moody Church.

His rallies, which were very similar in style to Moody's, were held in the United Kingdom, Australia, Japan, India, Canada, and China, and they only came to an end when failing health forced him to cancel a number of them the year before he died.

He was born in 1856 in Hoboken, New Jersey, and died in 1928 in Asheville, North Carolina.

His books include *What the Bible Teaches*, *How to Promote and Conduct a Successful Revival*, *The Gospel for Today*, and *Real Salvation and Whole-Hearted Service*.

☞

If we would get from God, we must give to others.

When we feel least like praying is the time when we most need to pray.

If we are to pray with power we must pray with faith.

The prayer that is born of meditation upon the Word of God is the prayer that soars upward most easily to God's listening ear.

More can be accomplished in prayer in the first hours of the day than at any other time during the day.

Nights of prayer to God are followed by days of power with men.

How to Pray (1900)

If any saved person will dwell long enough upon the peril and wretchedness of any man out of Christ and the worth of his soul in God's sight as seen in the death of God's Son to save him, a feeling of intense desire for that man's salvation is almost certain to follow.

The one who would have real success in bringing others to Christ must himself be *a thoroughly converted person*.

We must always bear in mind that the primary purpose of our work, is not to get persons to join the church or to give up their bad habits or to do anything else than this, to accept Jesus Christ as their Savior.

Every man's conscience is on our side.

A man's face will often reveal that which his words try to conceal.

There is no hope of bringing a man out of his delusion, unless he desires to know the truth.

By praying more we will not work any less and we will accomplish vastly more.

If there is any direction in which we are seeking to have our own way and not letting Him have His own way in our lives, our power will be crippled and men lost that we might have saved.

Among those who entertain false hopes, perhaps the largest class are those who expect to be saved by their righteous lives.

It is not so much God who damns men as men who damn themselves in spite of God's goodness because they will not come to Christ and accept the life freely offered.

How to Bring Men to Christ (1893)

TOZER, A. W.

Aiden Wilson Tozer was coming home from work when a street preacher said, "If you don't know how to be saved, just call on God, saying, 'Lord, be merciful to me, a sinner.'" Tozer made the call. And God answered.

At the age of twenty-two, Tozer pastored a storefront church in West Virginia, thus beginning a long association with the Christian and Missionary Alliance, which promoted higher standards in Christian life.

He often said that the modern church was in danger of being tainted by worldly matters. Living a simple life dedicated to prayer and preaching,

Tozer never owned a car and gave away much of the money he earned from his books to people in need.

Born in 1897 in Newburg, Pennsylvania, he died in 1963 in Toronto, Canada.

His books include *The Pursuit of God*, *The Knowledge of the Holy*, and *Man: The Dwelling Place of God*.

✍

If you go after the money and don't care about the people, we're hirelings and not shepherds.

When we pray more we can talk less.

"In Everything by Prayer" sermon (c. 1930)

People want the benefit of the cross but they do not want the control of the cross.

"Don't Beg God for the Holy Spirit" sermon (c. 1930)

It is doubtful whether God can bless a man greatly until He has hurt him deeply.

The Root of the Righteous (1955)

Regret for a sinful past will remain until we truly believe that for us in Christ that sinful past no longer exists.

By the power of the gospel the covetous man may become generous, the egotist lowly in his own eyes. The thief may learn to steal no more, the blasphemer to fill his mouth with praises unto God. But it is Christ who does it all.

That Incredible Christian (1960s)

The fellowship of the church has degenerated into a social fellowship with a mild religious flavor.

The Holy Spirit never enters a man and lets him live like the world. You can be sure of that.

"Who Is the Holy Spirit?" sermon (c. 1930)

With the goodness of God to desire our highest welfare, the wisdom of God to plan it, and the power of God to achieve it, what do we lack?

The greatness of God rouses fear within us, but His goodness encourages us not to be afraid of Him.

Knowledge of the Holy (1961)

Whoever defends himself will have himself for his defense, and he will have no other. But let him come defenseless before the Lord and he will have for his defender no less than God Himself.

The Pursuit of God (1948)

VERWER, GEORGE

Born in Ramsey, New Jersey, in 1938, George Verwer came to faith at the age of sixteen after hearing Billy Graham speak in Madison Square Garden. Three years later he and two friends began Operation Send the Light, sending copies of the Gospel of John to Mexico.

In 1961 Verwer went to Spain with his wife, Drena. While there they founded OM, or Operation Mobilization, which was dedicated to making disciples of young people and spreading the Gospel across the world.

Later Send the Light became involved in sending Christian material from the United Kingdom to India, and it is currently the largest distributor of Christian books in the UK.

His books include *Drops from a Leaking Tap*, *Out of the Comfort Zone*, *The Revolution of Love*, and *No Turning Back*.

✍

The Christian life is not a competition with others; we have a common goal and we grow together in the strength and grace of the body of believers.

Love is the essence of discipleship: it is the wall that surrounds a disciple, the roof that protects him, and the ground which supports him.

Come! Live! Die! (1972)

WARREN, RICK

Born in 1954 in San Jose, California, Rick Warren was doing God's work even while he was in high school when he and a few friends began the Fishers of Men Club at Ukiah High.

While at seminary he worked at the Texas Ranch for Christ. That was where he began writing about his faith. Arriving in Saddleback, California, in 1979, Rick and his wife, Kay, began a home Bible study with another couple. These humble beginnings grew into Saddleback Church, which now has around twenty thousand people attending each week.

In 2006 *Newsweek* included him in their list "15 People Who Make America Great." In 2008 he gave the invocation at the presidential inauguration ceremony.

His books include *The Purpose-Driven Church*, *The Purpose-Driven Life*, and *Answers to Life's Difficult Questions*.

✍

You are free to choose what you surrender to, but you are not free from the consequences of that choice.

Jesus did not die on the cross so we could have comfortable lives.

The Purpose-Driven Life (2002)

Jesus said, "You will know the truth, and the truth will set you free!" Lasting freedom from personal hang-ups comes from building our lives on the truth. Only the Bible can be depended on completely to provide truthful insights into the causes and cures for our personal problems.

God's Word has stood the test of time. It is just as relevant and applicable today as it was thousands of years ago. It contains the answers to life's most difficult questions.

God's Answers to Life's Difficult Questions (2006)

In the pursuit of a holier life during his college years, John Wesley, his brother Charles, and a few friends formed what came to be known as the Holy Club. They dedicated each waking hour to God, methodically carrying out good works and examining their own attitudes with a view to improving them. This "method" continued in his preaching, in which he encouraged everyone to strive for personal holiness and personal relationship with God. The Methodist movement was born and became a great force for social change in both Great Britain and the United States.

He was a lifelong Anglican despite that church's frequent disapproval of his activities. Later in life he became more accepted and was often referred to as "the best-loved man in England."

Born in 1703 in Epworth, England, he died in 1791 in London. His written works include *Notes on the New Testament* and *An Earnest Appeal to Men of Reason and Religion*.

✍

Here is knowledge enough for me. Let me be *homo unius libri* [a man of one book].

I design plain truth for plain people.

We may die without the knowledge of many truths, and yet be carried into Abraham's bosom. But, if we die without love, what will knowledge avail? Just as much as it avails the devil and his angels!

I have thought, I am a creature of a day, passing through life as an arrow through the air. I am a spirit come from God, and returning to God: Just hovering over the great gulf; till, a few moments hence, I am no more seen; I drop into an unchangeable eternity!

Sermons on Several Occasions (18th century)

Make haste. Eternity is at hand. Eternity depends on this moment. An eternity of happiness, or an eternity of misery!

Seest thou the necessity of that inward change, that spiritual birth, that life from the dead, that holiness? And art thou thoroughly convinced, that without it no man shall see the Lord?

Having no spiritual senses, no inlets of spiritual knowledge, the natural man receiveth not the things of the Spirit of God; nay, he is so far from receiving them, that whatsoever is spiritually discerned, is mere foolishness unto him. He is not content with being utterly ignorant of spiritual things, but he denies the very existence of them.

"Awake, Thou That Sleepest" sermon (1743)

This is the work which I know God has called me to; and sure I am that His blessing attends it.

Whoever sees me sees I would be a Christian. Therefore are my ways not like other men's ways.

His servant I am, and, as such, am employed according to the plain direction of His Word.

While he was describing the change which God works in the heart through faith in Christ, I felt my heart strangely warmed. I felt I did trust in Christ, Christ alone, for salvation; and an assurance was given me that He had taken away my sins, even mine, and saved me from the law of sin and death.

Whom then shall I hear, God or man?

There is but One, He that sitteth in heaven, who is able to teach man wisdom.

I look upon all the world as my parish; thus far I mean, that, in whatever part of it I am, I judge it meet, right, and my bounden duty to declare unto all that are willing to hear, the glad tidings of salvation.

The Journal of John Wesley (1738)

Therefore, in the name of God I exhort you, keep close every moment to the unction of the Holy One! Attend to the still, small voice! Beware of hearkening to the voice of a stranger!

"What do you want with me?" I want you, not to be a convert to my opinions, but to be a member of Christ, a child of God, and an heir of his kingdom.

Be active, be diligent; avoid all laziness, sloth, indolence. Fly from every degree, every appearance, of it; else you will never be more than half a Christian.

O speak nothing, act nothing, think nothing, but as you are taught of God!

Be anything, as to outward profession, so you are lowly in heart; so you resist and conquer every motion of pride, and have that mind in you which was also in Christ Jesus.

Yet I could not say, "Take thy plague away from me"; but only "Let me be purified, not consumed."

You must be much in the way, or much out of the way; a good soldier for God, or for the devil. O choose the better part—now!—today!

The Works of the Reverend John Wesley (1769)

None can trust in the merits of Christ, till he has utterly renounced his own.

Salvation by Faith (1738)

Good men avoid sin from the love of virtue: Wicked men avoid sin from a fear of punishment.

The Almost Christian (1741)

Take heed thou destroy not thy own soul by pleading thy righteousness more or less. Go as altogether ungodly, guilty, lost, destroyed, deserving and dropping into hell; and thou shalt then find favor in his sight, and know that he justifieth the ungodly.

Justifying faith implies, not only a divine evidence or conviction that "God was in Christ reconciling the world unto himself," but a sure trust and confidence that Christ died for my sins, that he loved me, and gave himself for me.

No works are good, which are not done as God hath willed and commanded them to be done.

Justification by Faith (1744)

Love is the fulfilling of the law, the end of the commandment.

Let your soul be filled with so entire a love to Him that you may love nothing but for His sake.

Desire not to live but to praise His name; let all your thoughts, words, and works tend to His glory.

This great gift of God, the salvation of our souls, is no other than the image of God fresh stamped on our hearts.

One design ye are to pursue to the end of time—the enjoyment of God in time and in eternity.

And where the Spirit of the Lord is, there is liberty; such liberty from the law of sin and death, as the children of this world will not believe, though a man declare it unto them.

A Plain Account of Christian Perfection (18th century)

I have frequently observed that there are two very different ranks of Christians, both of whom may be in the favor of God—a higher and a lower rank. The latter avoid all known sin, do much good, use all the means of grace, but have little of the life of God in their souls, but are much conformed to the world. The former make the Bible their whole rule, and their sole aim is the will and the image of God.

"Letter to Mr. _____" (1770)

Do you continually remind those under your care, that the one rational end of all our studies, is to know, love, and serve the only true God, and Jesus Christ whom He hath sent?

Scriptural Christianity (1744)

WHITEFIELD, GEORGE

Born in Gloucester, England, in 1714, George Whitefield was perhaps the most prominent voice in the Great Awakening of the 1830s and 1840s. Stressing a personal, life-changing relationship with a God who loved each person individually, Whitefield challenged the established church and rituals that often kept people distanced from God.

An open-air preacher, he also made good use of printed materials. After his evangelical tours of colonial America, it was estimated that around half of all Americans had either heard him speak or read his words in print.

While he was an orator and hymn writer, what we have by way of books from George Whitefield come mostly from his journals. These include *A Short Account of God's Dealings with the Reverend George Whitefield* and *A Further Account of God's Dealings with the Reverend George Whitefield*. He died in 1770 in Newburyport, Massachusetts.

For this life, being a continual warfare, we must never expect to have rest from our spiritual adversary the devil, or to say, our combat with him is finished, till, with our blessed master, we bow down our heads, and give up the ghost.

To check therefore all suggestions to spiritual pride, let us consider, that we did not apprehend Christ, but were apprehended of Him. That we have nothing but what we have received.

There is something so shocking in the consideration of eternal torments, and seemingly such an infinite disproportion between an endless duration of pain, and short life spent in pleasure, that men (some at least of them) can scarcely be brought to confess it as an article of their faith, that an eternity of misery awaits the wicked in a future state.

The torments reserved for the wicked hereafter, are eternal.

Consider, that it is necessary such inward trials should come, to wean us from the immoderate love of sensible devotion, and teach us to follow Christ, not merely for His loaves, but out of a principle of love and obedience.

If we would therefore behave like good soldiers of Jesus Christ, we must be always upon our guard, and never pretend to lay down our spiritual weapons of prayer and watching, till our warfare is accomplished by death.

There cannot be one argument urged, why God should reward His saints with everlasting happiness, which will not equally prove that He ought to punish sinners with eternal misery.

What [Satan] is most remarkable for is, his subtlety: for not having power given him from above, to take us by force, he is obliged to wait for opportunities to betray us, and to catch us by guile.

When persons are first awakened to the divine life, because grace is weak and nature strong, God is often pleased to vouchsafe them some extraordinary illuminations of His Holy Spirit; but when they are grown to be more perfect men in Christ, then he frequently seems to leave them to themselves; and not only so, but permits a horrible deadness and dread to overwhelm them; at which times Satan will not be wanting to vex and tempt them to impatience, to the great discomfort of their souls.

"All are not Israelites that are of Israel," so when applied to Christianity, all are not real Christians that are nominally such.

Selected Sermons of George Whitefield (c. 1738)

As God can send a nation or people no greater blessing, than to give them faithful, sincere, and upright ministers; so the greatest curse that God can possibly send upon a people in this world, is to give them over to blind, unregenerate, carnal, lukewarm, and unskilful guides.

"On the Method of Grace" sermon (1741)

If one evil thought, if one evil word, if one evil action, deserves eternal damnation; how many hells, my friends, do every one of us deserve, whose lives have been one continual rebellion against God?

Ye may do things materially good, but ye cannot do a thing formally and rightly good; because nature cannot act above itself. It is impossible that a man that is unconverted can act for the glory of God.

Before ye speak peace to your hearts, ye must be made to see, made to feel, made to weep over, made to bewail your actual transgressions against the law of God.

Know, by sad experience, what it is to be lulled asleep with a false peace. Long was I lulled asleep; long did I think myself a Christian, when I knew nothing of the Lord Jesus Christ.

Come away, my dear brethren, fly, fly, fly for your lives to Jesus Christ; fly to a bleeding God, fly to a throne of grace; and beg of God to break your heart; beg of God to convince you of your actual sins; beg of God to convince you of your original sin; beg of God to convince you of your self-righteousness; beg of God to give you faith, and to enable you to close with Jesus Christ.

My business this morning, the first day of the week, is to tell you that Christ is willing to be reconciled to you. Will any of you be reconciled to Jesus Christ?

I am grieved with the loose walk of those that are Christians, that have had discoveries of Jesus Christ; there is so little difference betwixt them and other people, that I can scarce know which is the true Christian.

God will not be mocked; that which a man soweth, that shall he also reap. And if ye will not be at peace with God, God will not be at peace with you. Who can stand before God when He is angry?

A Sermon, Preached on Sabbath Morning (1741)

Be humble, talk little, think and pray much.

If you must dispute, stay till you are master of the subject; otherwise you will hurt the cause you would defend.

Beware of a false peace: strive to enter in at the strait gate; and give all diligence to make your calling and election sure: remember you are but a babe in Christ, if so much!

Memoirs of Rev. George Whitefield (1741)

WIERSBE, WARREN

Born in 1929 in East Chicago, Indiana, Warren Wiersbe became a pastor while still attending Northern Baptist Theological Seminary. During his time at Calvary Baptist Church in Covington, he took the congregation from around eight hundred to two thousand and wrote the books that would become the basis for his "Be" series of Bible lessons. He wrote another twenty books while serving at the Moody Memorial Church in Chicago.

He taught at Trinity Evangelical Divinity School and produced the *Back to the Bible* radio program. Billy Graham described Warren Wiersbe as "one of the greatest Bible expositors of our generation."

His books include *The Twenty Essential Qualities of a Child of God*, *The Bumps Are What You Climb On*, *Lonely People*, and *Key Words of the Christian Life*.

What we know ourselves to be helps us behave the way we're supposed to behave.

The fact that we have our citizenship in heaven ought to make us better citizens on earth, no matter under what form of government we may live.

A Gallery of Grace (2002)

The Christian life is a pilgrimage from earth to heaven, and our task is to take as many as possible with us as we make this journey.

Witnessing for Christ is not something we turn on and off, like a TV set. Every believer is a witness at all times—either a good one or a bad one.

Be What You Are (1988)

The sin in our lives that we fail to conquer will eventually conquer us.

Be Available (1994)

WILKERSON, DAVID

David Wilkerson was born in Indiana in 1931 into a Bible-believing family and began preaching at the age of fourteen. He was preaching in Pennsylvania when an article on gangs in New York led him to move to that city. There he began a street ministry reaching out to addicts and gang members. The story of his time on the streets, *The Cross and the Switchblade*, became a bestseller. It is listed in *Christianity Today*'s "50 Books That Have Shaped Evangelicals."

In addition to Teen Challenge, he founded Youth Crusade, which led to CURE Corps, Times Square Church, and World Challenge, an organization set up to reach the world with the Gospel.

He died in Texas in 2011.

His books include *The Cross and the Switchblade*, *David Wilkerson Exhorts the Church*, *When in Doubt. . . Faith It*, and *Hungry for More of Jesus*.

✍

Our faith is not meant to get us out of a hard place or change our painful condition. Rather, it is meant to reveal God's faithfulness to us in the midst of our dire situation.

God does at times change our trying circumstances. But more often, He doesn't—because He wants to change us!

"Have Faith in God's Faithfulness" article (2009)

True freedom from fear consists of totally resigning one's life into the hands of the Lord.

"Resigned into God's Care" sermon (2010)

"To die is gain!" (Philippians 1:21). That kind of talk is absolutely foreign to our modern, spiritual vocabularies. We have become such life worshippers, we have very little desire to depart to be with the Lord.

Death is but a mere breaking of the fragile shell.

"The Life Is Not in the Shell" sermon (2010)

Even Jesus wept in His trying hour; He knows our pain firsthand.

As far as the Lord is concerned, the time to stand is in the darkest moment. It is when everything seems hopeless, when there appears no way out, when God alone can deliver.

"Right Song, Wrong Side" sermon (2009)

We all have seeds of jealousy and envy in us. The question is, who among us will acknowledge it?

"Seeds of Envy and Jealousy" article (2009)

The accuser of the brethren waits, like a vulture, for you to fail in some way.

Something much worse than failure is the fear that goes with it.

Don't Be Afraid of Failure (2009)

The hardest part of faith is the last half hour.

World Challenge Pulpit Series (c. 2000)

Godly patience is a willingness to wait for God's timing.

All the human abilities in the world won't bring down a single stronghold of Satan.

The Lord is determined to strip us of all confidence in the flesh, leaving us with total confidence in Him.

"Hold On to Your Confidence" article (2010)

A humble person is not one who thinks little of himself, hangs his head and says, "I'm nothing." Rather, he is one who depends wholly on the Lord for everything, in every circumstance.

At its heart, legalism is a desire to appear holy. It is trying to be justified before men and not God.

Revival on Broadway! (1996)

Obedience reflects belief.

"The Ultimate Test of Faith" article (2009)

Be specific with God in prayer and He will be specific with you in regard to the answer.

"Prayer—The Long and Short of It!" article (2009)

Come boldly into His throne of grace—even when you have sinned and failed. He forgives—instantly—those who repent with godly sorrow.

Thank God, suffering is always that short period before final victory.

"A Dry Spell" article (2010)

WILKINSON, BRUCE

Early in his career Bruce Wilkinson, who was born in 1940 in New Jersey, served as a professor at Multnomah Bible School. He left Multnomah to set up the parachurch organization Walk Thru the Bible, an organization that has now trained seminar instructors in more than ninety countries.

In 1998 he founded WorldTeachers, an organization set up with the goal of eventually providing one Bible teacher for every fifty thousand people in the world. His book *You Were Born for This* suggests and teaches that Christians can and should expect to be delivery people for God's miracles on a near-daily basis. He also served on the overview committee for the New King James Bible.

His books include *You Were Born for This*, *Almost Every Answer for Practically Any Teacher*, *Personal Holiness in Times of Temptation*, and *The Prayer of Jabez*.

☞

Our God specializes in working through normal people who believe in a supernormal God who will do His work through them.

God's bounty is limited only by us, not by His resources, power, or willingness to give.

The Prayer of Jabez (2000)

If you stay connected to Him, if you draw spiritual nourishment from Him, if you allow the power that flows through Him to flow through you, nothing will hold you back from reaching the most abundant life possible.

God didn't want me to do more for Him. He wanted me to be more with Him.

Secrets of the Vine (2001)

The way of the dreamer is difficult—but anything less is hardly living at all!

Until you decide to pursue your dream, you are never going to love your life the way you were meant to.

The Dream Giver (2003)

God wants you to enjoy His blessings—and to use them to make a difference in the world around you.

Enlarge my territory. I encourage you to pray this for all of your God-honoring pursuits. Much of what God wants us to do involves the expansion of not only literal territory, but influence as well.

Beyond Jabez (2005)

When we actively seek to expand His life in ours, His character gradually becomes ours.

All of Christ's reasons for loving the church are concerned with what He can do for the church, not with what the church does for Him.

Experiencing Spiritual Breakthroughs (1999)

Your choices on earth have direct consequences on your life in eternity.

Jesus will not love you any less or any more for all eternity than He loved you when He purchased your life with His own blood.

A Life God Rewards (2002)

WILLARD, DALLAS

Born in 1935 in St. Louis, Missouri, Dallas Willard was a spiritual philosopher who once claimed to be on a quiet crusade to subvert nominal Christianity. His passion was to encourage people to be disciples of Christ in the way an apprentice might emulate a craftsman and do his best to be like him. This was possible, he believed, through focusing on and developing the fruits of the Spirit.

He was professor of philosophy at the University of Southern California and chair of the department in the mid-eighties. His last words before he died in 2013 were "Thank you."

His books include *Renovations of the Heart: Putting On the Character of Christ, The Great Omission: Reclaiming Jesus' Essential Teachings on Discipleship,* and *Knowing Christ Today: Why We Can Trust Spiritual Knowledge.*

☞

The correct perspective is to see following Christ not only as the necessity it is, but as the fulfillment of the highest human possibilities and as life on the highest plane.

The cross-shaped yoke of Christ is after all an instrument of liberation and power to those who live in it with him and learn the meekness and lowliness of heart that brings rest to the soul.

The Spirit of the Disciplines (1988)

YANCEY, PHILIP

Born in Atlanta, Georgia, in 1948, Philip Yancey's childhood was one of con-tradictions when it came to faith. The Christianity and the God he was taught often seemed quite different from the one he experienced daily. A passion for reading provided him with another viewpoint and an increased understand-ing. But he has been asking questions ever since and finding a ready audience for his answers.

After graduating from college he spent twenty years as a journalist. He went on to become editor of *Christianity Today.*

His refuge and inspiration is the Bible, where he says all the difficult questions about faith have already been asked—and answered. He is accustomed to various reactions to his books and says he speaks to those living in the borderlands of faith.

His books include *What Good Is God?*, *What's So Amazing about Grace?*, and *The Jesus I Never Knew*.

✍

The Bible never belittles human disappointment, but it does add one key word: temporary. What we feel now, we will not always feel.

Disappointment with God (1992)

What makes us human is not our mind but our heart, not our ability to think but our ability to love.

Grace is absolute, inflexible, all-encompassing.

The Jesus I Never Knew (1995)

Prayer allows a place for me to bring my doubts and complaints and subject them to the blinding light of reality I cannot comprehend but can haltingly learn to trust.

If I started with the mind and will of God, viewing the rest of my life from that point of view, other details would fall into place—or at least fall into a different place.

Prayer: Does It Make Any Difference? (2006)

The world thirsts for grace in ways it does not even recognize; little wonder the hymn "Amazing Grace" edged its way onto the Top Ten charts two hundred years after composition.

Grace is Christianity's best gift to the world, a spiritual nova in our midst exerting a stronger force than vengeance, stronger than racism, stronger than hate.

What's So Amazing about Grace? (1997)

Pain is not an afterthought, or God's great goof. Rather, it reveals a marvelous design that serves our bodies well. Pain is as essential to a normal life, it could be argued, as eyesight or even good circulation.

Where Is God When It Hurts? (2002)

Because of Jesus we need never question God's desire for intimacy. Does God really want close contact with us? Jesus gave up heaven for it. In person He reestablished the original link between God and human beings, between seen and unseen worlds.

What difference did Jesus make? Both for God and for us, He made possible an *intimacy* that had never before existed.

Grace Notes (2009)

Christians are not perfect, by any means, but they can be people made fully alive.

We admit that we will never reach our ideal in this life, a distinctive the church claims that most other human institutions try to deny.

Soul Survivor: How My Faith Survived the Church (2002)

We are all trophies of God's grace, some more dramatically than others; Jesus came for the sick and not the well, for the sinner and not the righteous. He came to redeem and transform, to make all things new. May you go forth more committed than ever to nourish the souls who you touch, those tender lives who have sustained the enormous assaults of the universe.

I go to church as an expression of my need for God and for God's family.

What Good Is God? In Search of a Faith That Matters (2010)

Jesus gave us a model for the work of the church at the Last Supper. While His disciples kept proposing more organization—Hey, let's elect officers, establish hierarchy, set standards of professionalism—Jesus quietly picked up a towel and basin of water and began to wash their feet.

As I look around on Sunday morning at the people populating the pews, I see the risk that God has assumed. For whatever reason, God now reveals Himself in the world not through a pillar of smoke and fire, not even through the physical body of His Son in Galilee, but through the mongrel collection that comprises my local church and every other such gathering in God's name.

Church: Why Bother? My Personal Pilgrimage (2001)

I have found that living with faith in an unseen world requires constant effort.

Rumors of Another World: What on Earth Are We Missing? (2003)

God reproduces and lives out His image in millions of ordinary people like us. It is a supreme mystery. We are called to bear that image as a Body because any one of us taken individually would present an incomplete image, one partly false and always distorted, like a single glass chip hacked from a mirror. But collectively, in all our diversity, we can come together as a community of believers to restore the image of God in the world.

In His Image (with Dr. Paul Brand, 1987)

Pleasure represents a great good but also a grave danger.

As the books of Job, Jeremiah, and Habakkuk clearly show, God has a high threshold of tolerance for what is appropriate to say in a prayer. God can "handle" my unsuppressed rage. I may well find that my vindictive feelings need God's correction—but only by taking those feelings to God will I have the opportunity for correction and healing.

The Bible Jesus Read: An 8-Session Exploration of the Old Testament (2002)

In no other arena is the church at greater risk of losing its calling than in the public square.

Christians and Politics: Uneasy Partners (2012)

On a small scale, person-to-person, Jesus encountered the kinds of suffering common to all of us. And how did He respond? Avoiding philosophical theories and theological lessons, He reached out with healing and compassion. He forgave sin, healed the afflicted, cast out evil, and even overcame death.

The Question That Never Goes Away (2014)

ZACHARIAS, RAVI

Born in Chennai, India, in 1946, Ravi Zacharias (Frederick Antony Ravi Kumar Zacharias) was an atheist until the age of seventeen. While he was recovering in the hospital from an unsuccessful suicide attempt, his mother read to him from the Bible. The words changed his life. He went on to become, in the words of Chuck Colson, "the great apologist of our time."

In the eighties he began to notice a lack of effective modern Christian apologetics in a particular area. As a result he now focuses his message toward those who consider themselves too educated for faith.

Ravi Zacharias International Ministries has offices in Canada, England, India, Singapore, and the United Arab Emirates.

His books include *A Shattered Visage: The Real Face of Atheism, Jesus among Other Gods,* and *Who Made God? And Answers to Over 100 Other Tough Questions of Faith.*

☜

Having killed God, the atheist is left with no reason for being, no morality to espouse, no meaning to life, and no hope beyond the grave.

The farther we move from God, the more we devalue man.

The Real Face of Atheism (2004)

Only God is able to humble us without humiliating us and to exalt us without flattering us.

Like a child who suddenly stops sobbing when he is clasped in the arms of his mother, such will be the grip of heaven upon our souls.

Recapture the Wonder (2003)

When God brings us to salvation, the most remarkable thing we see is that He transforms our hungers. He changes not just what we do but what we want to do.

To allow God to be God we must follow Him for who He is and what He intends, and not for what we want and what we prefer.

The Grand Weaver (2007)

Generally, there is one desire or one habit that keeps us from enjoying and tasting the fullness of God.

"Is There Not a Cost?" sermon (2008)

The primary purpose of a home is to reflect and to distribute the love of Christ. Anything that usurps that is idolatrous.

Young dreams may be wild ones, but they are never corrected by ridiculing them. They must be steered by a loving voice that has earned the right to be heard, not one enforced by means of power.

Jesus among Other Gods (2000)

The greatest obstacle to the impact of the gospel has not been its inability to provide answers, but the failure on our part to live it out.

If the concept of sin doesn't make sense, then someone dying for our sins is even more confusing and considered downright ridiculous by many.

Beyond Opinion (2007)

One of the most dangerous and terrifying trends in America today is the disregard for character as a central necessity in a leader's credentials.

The constant bombardment of images shapes the perceptions of a whole generation and results in altered beliefs and lifestyles that make even the aberrant seem normal.

Deliver Us from Evil (1996)

After two thousand years, no name has been scrutinized more, none abused or challenged more in the public media.

I find a lot of Western journalists intellectually cowardly here. They would never do with Mohammed what they do with Jesus.

Christian Worldview (2008)

You hear it a thousand times and more growing up in the East—"We all come through different routes and end up in the same place." But I say to you, God is not a place or an experience or a feeling.

Pluralistic cultures are beguiled by the cosmetically courteous idea that sincerity or privilege of birth is all that counts and that truth is subject to the beholder.

What Is Truth? (2007)

The denial of an objective moral law, based on the compulsion to deny the existence of God, results ultimately in the denial of evil itself.

Our inability to alter what is actual frustrates our grandiose delusions of being sovereign over everything.

"The Undeluded Truth?" article (2008)

Jesus makes an amazing statement. He not only claims to be unique and to have the power to transform anyone who comes to Him, but the Bible says we are "made complete" in Him (Colossians 2:10).

There is a war raging. It is the battle for thought and belief through a weapon of mass destruction. In that battle, it is not firepower we need to fear as much as it is electronic power.

Why Jesus? (2012)

Once we understand Jesus in His *own* words and measure His claims and promises against our deepest needs, we will be surprised at just how personal and magnificent He really is.

The spiritual talk of today is all about feelings and ideas; Jesus' message, on the other hand, is about the person and presence of God.

Has Christianity Failed You? (2010)

When we learn God's profound answers to every sentiment we feel, we find contentment and courage and live a life of hope and confidence.

In His grace and wisdom, God has blessed us with intellects and senses that long to see, to hear, and to know Him.

Cries of the Heart (2002)

Through technology the whole world has now become the media's parish, talk-show hosts the prophets, actors and musicians the priests, and any script will do for the scriptures as long as moral constraints are removed.

Can Man Live without God? (1994)

Love is a commitment that will be tested in the most vulnerable areas of spirituality, a commitment that will force you to make some very difficult choices. It is a commitment that demands that you deal with your lust, your greed, your pride, your power, your desire to control, your temper, your patience, and every area of temptation that the Bible clearly talks about. It demands the quality of commitment that Jesus demonstrates in His relationship to us.

Unless I understand the Cross, I cannot understand why my commitment to what is right must take precedence over what I prefer.

I, Isaac, Take Thee, Rebekah: Moving from Romance to Lasting Love (2005)

I thank the Lord that, even though things were so wrong in my life here, I finally was brought to the realization of what all those struggles were about. There are some wonderful things from your painful past, things with a beauty you may not have realized at the time.

Walking from East to West: God in the Shadows (2006)